Chop wood, Carry water

Section One

Live Long & Prosper

1

Once a week I peel off all my skin and climb on top of the Naples Daily News building. I then proceed to shout at the top of my lungs about topics that are never ensured a warm welcome. Yoga, philosophy, theology—things we are currently dissuaded from speaking about in polite company. Yep. That's me up there, the lunatic fringe, bucking social convention with a bullhorn.

To my never ending surprise and delight, people respond. For the most part positively. That simple support keeps my courage strong as I put those rebel thoughts out there into the world. But sometimes, people respond negatively. I take equal pleasure in the dissenting opinion for it is those who abjectly disagree that keep me thinking about what I say and why I say it. It is those few who keep me absolutely genuine.

I was recently assaulted (verbally) by someone who took extreme objection to my willingness to believe something that could not be proven. In a nutshell, my intelligence was questioned—and my integrity—because I asked others to believe the same.

We live in an era of science. A time when everything has its place and its explanation. Nothing is real until our scientists to prove it valid. And then we accept it wholesale, rarely questioning the result. Until it bites us in the butt. And then we usually shrug it off, confident that another batch of scientists will right the wrong.

Heaven forfend we take anything on faith. And I don't mean the kind of faith that comes in a tent. I mean that deep, abiding faith in the unseen world. The world of ideas and grace. The world that generates love and peace. This unseen world is intangible. You cannot ever prove it exists—although quantum physics may be getting close. And still, those who study quantum often say that they find themselves heeling faith.

To try and bring this other world strictly into the confines of our physical realm is impossible. It will always exist only within our minds and our spirits. It cannot ever be separated out. This unseen world is the very foundation on which we build our humanity. So, while it may be a scientific, genetically proven fact that we are just upright apes, it is this unseen world of faith, grace and love that makes us ever so much more.

Why on earth would anyone dream of proving grace? Does it fit into a Petri dish? Can it be saved to a hard drive? If we all waited for the scientific authority to validate grace, we would be left waiting in a very cold world. To minimize the value of grace because it cannot be proven is to debunk Jesus and other figures like him. It is to crush the archetypal standards with which we navigate our way through the dark tunnels of human need. We need grace, proven or not.

What about love? It can't be charted. Love just is. It is completely ethereal and yet find me one person on the face of this green earth who is waiting for science to prove that love exists. Maybe science will determine the chemical that makes love—but who wants to see love reduced to a neurotransmitter? Love is as necessary to our lives as water; we don't need it proven to us.

Ideas, memory, dreams, spirit, soul—our very essence—these are all things that belong in our unseen world. Nobody, nobody needs scientific study to prove that they are real. Quite simply, proof is not the point. Proof can be wrong. Proof can be fixed. The things that matter, that which makes us remarkable, will never, ever, be scientific provenance.

Maybe I am a fool for believing. But I would far rather be a faithful fool than a blind one.

2

I just read an interesting parable that had to do with the process of enlightenment. It was about a master and a student, eating rice from a bowl. The student asks the master what else he should be doing to move along his path to enlightenment. The master asks him if he has finished his rice. The student replies in the affirmative. The master then tells him to wash out his bowl.

That's it. That was his answer to the question. "Wash out your bowl." Brilliant.

This sort of irreverent description of the enlightenment quest is brilliant simply because it is so useable. So accessible. I have no idea how it became this way, but our current, common image of 'enlightenment' is a strangely limited one. Just the very word conjures up old men on mountaintops, or monks in caves, loincloths, robes, and above all else—quixotic solitude interrupted by only the most disciplined of seekers. It seems that renunciation, withdrawal and enlightenment must go hand in hand. And let us not forget all that communing with God that goes on up there in the clouds and produces only deep, thoughtful riddles that can be deciphered only with careful meditation and intense concentration. Am I right?

Jeez. As it is currently perceived, enlightenment seems like darned serious work. Too serious for me, I must say. My life is messy and full; I don't have time for riddles or mountain hiking. Lucky for me (and you) that the image of enlightenment is so very far from the reality of it and truth can be found quite easily. Right now.

This small parable makes it quite clear that growing enlightenment finds success in simply doing what comes next. You are here. It is now. Finding enlightenment means not turning the quest for it into a production, but being with it as it unfolds. If you act in this manner all the time, you move your awareness into present time. You begin to see moment to moment. And any moment, when examined or endured on its own without the chain of friends that usually accompany it, is as light as air. All on its own, any moment is filled with it's own enlightened grace.

All of life is but a series of these moments, strung together like sacred *mala* beads. Your fingers brush them for as long as it takes to breathe a prayer and then you have moved on. That breath has passed, everything that that breath may have represented has passed as well. That moment, that thought, that experience—no matter how good or bad—is gone. And then you encounter another bead, a different breath, a new prayer.

Every moment is a fresh opportunity to unfold into enlightened thinking. Sometimes we do it with grace; sometimes we do it with curses. But if we can let go of what was, forsake the expectation of what might be, and be present with the moment at hand we just might find that moment filled with true bliss. An instant of eternal insight. Enlightenment is nothing more than finding each instant ripe with God's peace. Enlightenment lives in dirty dishes as well as on mountaintops, in instants as well as eternity.

Those wonderful moments are just waiting to emerge when our hands are full of everyday things. Peace is riding shotgun every moment of every day. Enlightenment has been in your pocket for years. But if you relegate it to a role separate from the mundane, you'll never find it. No matter how far up the mountain you climb, or how many sages you ask.

There, now, grasshopper. Go clean out your bowl.

3

It is very easy to talk about yoga as simply a physical practice. It is only somewhat easy to speak of how those physical aspects translate into mental and emotional realization. It is downright hard to communicate the deeper principles of yoga, especially when they fly in the face of our cultural norms. The very valuable lesson of Attachment is one example of this difficult juxtaposition.

As Americans, we are encouraged to succeed. We are told in a hundred subtle ways that, should we strive for success, we will find happiness. Even worse, our personal worth is determined by how well we manage this type of success. Just over there, just a little bit further, just a little more work, just a few more moments away and we shall be blissfully worthy. We hinge so much of ourselves on a possibility that lives off in the distant future because that is how our culture functions. We are, at heart, a civilization of gamblers always banking on future earnings.

As yogis, we are encouraged to release ourselves from this method of thinking and being. A bedrock philosophy of the practice, non-attachment to things, people, ideas, and egos is how we are taught to find happiness. In other words, one cannot know what will happen at any other time than right now, so it is asking for upset to become attached to possibility. Once utilized, this method of being is quite liberating. But getting there is a hell of a trick.

To let go of an expected outcome is tough. That is because this is where our dreams live—off in the land of maybe, possibly, hopefully. We have all been taught to follow our dreams. We have all been taught to live in the possibility of tomorrow, oftentimes at the expense of today. Like a rusty safety pin, or a drunken gambler, we are stuck in the hope of a big happiness payoff and can't get free of it. This hope is so bright that it can easily obscure reality and leave us in the lurch.

Attaching ideas of personal success or failure, worth or significance—and all of the emotions that accompany them—to something that has no real substance is a really bad idea. When you do this, you are playing roulette with your peace of mind. Real problems may be neglected as your eyes are turned to possible rewards. How can happiness ever come out of that?

We can't know absolutely what the results of our actions will be. Any decision, even a wise one, has the potential to take off on a wild hair and go in a direction completely unexpected. It isn't smart to invest in what you think might possibly be what could happen. This is, as my grandmother says, "borrowing trouble."

We can only trust in what happens right now. From that all clarity flows. No one is suggesting that you don't follow your dreams. We wouldn't be human if we didn't dream. But one must always be aware of the present situation so that we can sense when that dream is failing us. Just because you have always dreamed of being a dancer does not mean that you will dance in Carnegie Hall. If you have pinned your very identity to that dream, what happens to you when it doesn't come? What if it was never meant to be? What joy could you have missed along the way by attaching the value of success to a task you love?

Sometimes possibilities are poisons that keep us from truly finding ourselves. Disattach from them and be content with who you are and where you are. Take joy in the doing and leave it at that.

Because castles made of air tend to blow away.

4

I made a friend in college who was the undisputed King of Theories. Quite independent of his formal studies, this man thought about and pondered everything under the sun. Looking back, I can see it was a blessing that I met and knew him and that I was afforded the opportunity to bandy about a few 'theories' of my own at an age when ideas about life and living take firm root.

This man was the first philosopher-poet I had ever met. I hope somewhere along the course of your experience that you have known one, too. They are invaluable guides.

One of his more practical theories had to do with the use of the body's energy supply. Long before I knew what yoga was or what it could do, this friend introduced me to the idea that the body was more than just a physical vehicle and it was more than just food that made it run. He believed that the body had a finite energy supply ("joules", he called them) and that you were only allotted so much energy every day. Now, according to this theory, you could borrow against future days, but you would eventually go into 'energy debt'. This created fatigue, irritability, and sickness. If you follow this theory to the end, one could say that going into extreme energy debt would shorten your life.

Now, whether you think this is hooey or not, just follow me for a moment. We all know that Stress is the new Satan and the stressful way we live our lives—busy in body, busy in mind, absent in spirit—is the root of our problems. But what is stress, really, but the body's engines running in the red all day long? Stress is this energy debt and we are maxing out our energy charge cards every day that we live so thoughtlessly. If we only have so much energy to spend, and we spend it foolishly by trying to 'do it all', what are we giving up? How much of our lives are we wasting by spinning around, never maximizing where we are?

I can't tell you how to spend your energy just as I can't tell you how to spend your money (…organic foods, free-trade products, eco-friendly goods…). But I can try to demonstrate how you are perhaps wasting your valuable resources.

I find, of course, that yoga class is a great example of this. It is, truly, life in microcosm. Some students come in and find their one-pointed focus, practicing with an economy of motion that refreshes and revitalizes. These people spend very little of their energy supply—even in a vigorous practice. Others come in and fidget. Their eyes dart about. They pick at their toes, rub their legs, bounce their knees. They wriggle about into the postures, never quite finding the stillpoint. These people are throwing their energy pennies down the well, wishing for peace.

We behave this way every day, either performing our tasks with focus and intention, or with scattered effort. When we do what needs to be done without any drama, one task at a time, we do not deplete ourselves. No matter how much we do. No matter what we do. But when we whirl about, trying to do seventeen things at once without presence, we waste ourselves and begin to borrow from tomorrow.

You must focus as you act. Be aware of your tasks and how you manage them. Sort out the important from the mere busy. Know, without a doubt, how much of your action—physical, mental, spiritual—is necessary. And how much is, in the words of another philosopher-poet, "Sound and fury… signifying nothing."

In this way, we can all live long and prosper.

5

Ah, yes.

The Wheel has turned and once again we find ourselves with an opportunity to re-align ourselves with the way of nature. The 21st/ 22nd of March is the Vernal Equinox, one of two points in the year when the Earth comes to balance. Here we come to a state in which the day and the night are equally as long.

This Equinox, the Spring Equinox, is a time to enjoy growing warmth, increasing light, and the time of beginnings. In olden times, this date was the marker for spring planting; it was time to put seeds in the ground. For our own modern times, it is a chance to find our own state of balance, internal and external. It is an opportunity to take a breath, set things on the right course and them let them go with complete faith that they will find their way to fruition.

Now, that's a tricky one. We do like to drive the events of our lives here in America. The act of trusting our fates to the, well, Fates is not something that we do well.

But look back, if you will, at all of the times you tinkered with something, hoping to make it better and ending up with a mess. Remember a time when your actions actually hindered the process whereas, had you left well enough alone, it might have flourished. We do this with such ease. It is part of our nature. Life is like a tree, a slow grower sensitive to equilibrium. An incessant re-working of life can throw it out of tune, just like too much kneading will ruin the rise of the dough.

You have to keep yourself in balance. Know when to act and when to leave well enough alone. This is the lesson of nature. This is the opportunity to be found in the Equinox.

It is an issue of trust and faith. The ancients trusted that if they put seeds in the ground at this time and treated them according to the rules of nature, they would grow. They had faith that there would be crops as long as certain observances were maintained. These were simple ideas. Action and restraint created the results they desired. Do the right thing at the right time and then wait.

Is this something you can say about yourself? Or are you one of those that believes nothing will go right unless you keep at it, keep working it, keep shaping it?

The art of release is a tough one to master because its counterpoint is so very, very dangerous. Take away the first half of the equation, the action, and you are left waiting for a ship that will never come in. To do nothing is much more treacherous than doing too much. If you don't plant the seed, or knead the dough, you're going to end up very hungry. Doing nothing creates nothing. One cannot exist on a life of nothing. You must, simply must, participate.

So how do you know when to act and when to wait? The answer, grasshopper, is balance. Balance, attention and trust. You must know what action is right to make and what attention it requires. Then set things in motion and believe that you have done what is necessary to let the laws of physics play their part. External or internal, things in motion tend to stay in motion. As long as you don't put obstacles in the path, and nurture without meddling, things will most likely turn out as they should. The Universe really is on your side.

Now is the time to create that which you want to grow. Make it happen and allow it to happen. Equinox reminds us that balance is a natural state of affairs. Tricky. But eminently possible.

Unlike up north, I find that the passage of seasons in Naples, Florida is not marked by temperature, color or clothing, but by automobiles. When I see a preponderance of Mercedes on the road, I think to myself, "Why, it must be October." When those Mercedes are joined by Bentleys, Rolls Royces and Jaguars, I can say with surety that it is January and 'season' has begun.

As I navigate my way through these expensive cars in my Chitty-Chitty-Bang-Bang of a Toyota, it is hard not to feel some envy. These drivers must be very successful to own such lavish cars. They must have an excess of wealth to spend it so freely on such a utilitarian possession. They must be highly prosperous. (Or highly in debt.) It is difficult not to compare my possession to theirs and find theirs—for a moment--so much better than mine.

Good thing that envy only lasts for a flash before I come to my senses. Truly, even if I had three hundred thousand dollars, I wouldn't spend it on a Rolls. But, hey, that's me, my blue collar upbringing, and my yogic philosophy at play. Because I know that true prosperity has absolutely no relationship to money.

You can be the most prosperous person in the world without a dollar in your pocket. You can have everything you need—and more--without having a lush stock portfolio. You can be rich beyond measure without owning a big, showy house. Because prosperity is not a physical manifestation, but rather a state of being. Prosperity is when the mind and heart are at peace with the universe, when gratitude sits in the front seat and when the spirit is open and willing to receive the true gifts of life.

Unlike simple, worldly wealth, prosperity is a flow. It needs space to move into. It doesn't stick around and gather dust. The principle of prosperity is that you get what you need when you need it. And, if you lock your mind into the belief that only money makes you rich, then you are inhibiting the flow of true prosperity into your life. One's focus needs to move away from money equals prosperity and into love equals prosperity. Or, luck equals prosperity. Or, joy equals prosperity. Or belonging equals prosperity. I could go on, but I am sure you take my meaning.

Don't believe the media hype. You cannot buy satisfaction. Prosperity is not imprinted over Benjamin Franklin's face, or woven into the leather stitching of a Gucci bag. Prosperity shows itself when you are open to receiving what you need, *in whatever form it takes.* Don't pigeonhole yourself by assuming that only possessions of status will make you happy, fulfilled or prosperous. It is a dangerous trap that limits your possibilities for joy and wealth.

So, maybe my Toyota burps up a little smoke now and then. But it has carried me through many life-enhancing journeys and for that I am grateful. I may not have a stock portfolio, but it would take all of my fingers and all of my toes—maybe even a few of yours—to count all of the people who truly, honestly love me. And, perhaps my house would only feel spacious to Barbie, but the love of the man who shares it with me is beyond space and measure.

At this precise moment, I have $2.18 in my cash purse--plus a strange Italian coin (how did that get there?) --but I count myself among the richest and most prosperous people in the world. Lucky, lucky me.

I sincerely, with all of my heart and more, wish the same for you.

7

Have you ever had a sublime experience?

I recently found myself smack dab in the middle of one. Somewhere between Bird-in-Hand and Intercourse, Pennsylvania, on rural route 340 heading east I discovered something divine. Tears came to my eyes. I was overwhelmed with emotion—happiness, confusion, relief. I thought for a moment that I was losing my grip.

It took me a moment to realize that what I was feeling was that unique instant when everything comes together and life is simply perfect. I was in the exact right place, at the exact right time, doing exactly what I wanted to be doing with exactly the right music, the exact right scenery, the exact right mindset. Stunned by the magnificence of the moment, I may have forgotten to breathe. It was a convergence of so many things that made me happy, so many things that made me me, that I couldn't help but to be moved.

It was fantastic.

I think I can safely say, however, that I never would have experienced this shining example of perfect joy had I not been a practitioner of yoga. I've driven these same roads before. I've seen the scenery. I've heard that CD countless times. But they have never moved me to tears. Had I not known how to be in the moment, to be present in all things, I very well may have missed it. And that would have been tragic.

We spend so much time waiting for the perfect moment when we think we can finally be happy. We try to craft it or to force it. "I'll be happy when…" Go ahead and fill in the blank here, we all do it. I'll be happy when I get that promotion. I'll be happy when I find a partner. I'll be happy when I have that baby. Nobody ever says, "I'll be truly happy when I don't expect it, driving down a country road."

Life's joys happen when they happen, not when we decide that they can happen. Happiness is not attached to anything specific, or at least not the kind of happiness that travels with the sublime. I've discovered here that real, transcendental happiness is like a lightening bolt. You don't know where it is going to come from, or when. You have to be open to it every moment of every day. And, generally, if you spend time shaping it, you probably won't find it.

The joy that is part and parcel of our human experience is a gift. We have to be willing to receive it no matter what shape or form it takes. It is pot luck. It is a grab bag. It is a butterfly on the wind. If you release control of what you think will make you happy, you might be surprised at what ends up doing just that. It is a beautiful thing when we learn to be open and grateful to any little thing. It is even more beautiful when we allow that little thing to move us into the presence of the sublime.

Then we have truly found ourselves in the presence of god. And lets not forget, my dears, that god lives in the trees, in the wind, in our hearts. If we open ourselves up to the moment, we will find more in that fraction of time than we ever dreamed. Joy, beauty, peace, happiness, the very essence of life. Those sublime experiences are so rare because we think far too much about what they ought to be. They are simple and perfect gifts that we unwrap just by being present with ourselves in the flow of life.

I found perfect joy on route 340. Go figure. Where could you find it?

If you have ever listened to the teachings of the Dalai Lama, you will understand that his entire mission is about compassion. He believes that all humans are capable of compassion and, by expressing it, we can turn the course of humanity.

What a lovely idea.

Where that concept gets bumpy is in most people's perception of compassion. All too often this generous emotion translates into pity. Pity, when distilled, has roots in judgement that miss the mark of compassion entirely.

So what exactly is compassion, then? And how do we find it? Compassion grows from the seeds of empathy. Not sympathy. Empathy. That sense of "that could be me." Or, better yet, "that is me." Compassion comes from realizing that we are all human, and, on the deepest (or highest, if you like) level we are all the same. We are all traveling through a life experience. For some it is a prosperous existence. For others it is one of troubles. Compassion is realizing that a different path of experience does not make one person better than the other. Compassion is knowing that all people are worthy of happiness, regardless of how different they are from you. Compassion is developing the ability to love without convenient restraint.

Developing compassion is often a difficult challenge. There are people in the world who do bad things. But compassion can't pick and choose because then it slides down the slippery slope of judgement. We are taught in so many subtle ways to look down on others. Not consciously, not with awareness, but we create rifts between ourselves and others based on social differences, economic & cultural differences, or differing beliefs. How easy it would be to qualify compassion based on what we believe is worthy of it. This subtle belief of "look out for your own" paralyzes compassion and neglects the larger picture.

In order for the world to change you must love everybody as you love yourself.

And I don't mean that you have to give every stranger a big fat hug and kiss. But you do have to believe, with every kernel of your being that

that person—no matter how different, how difficult or misguided—has a right to live. Better yet, they have a right to love. Without that belief, without compassion, we will tear this whole world to bits and find ourselves out of luck in terms of survival.

So, the next time you are out and about, maybe in the Post Office, the mall or Starbucks, practice your compassion. Standing in the crowd, open your heart and look at all of the people around you. Feel, for just a moment, the thread of love that connects you to them. Pick out one person and have compassion for them. Look at how they walk or stand, read their face, their body language, look at their eyes. Make no judgement, but experience that person as if it were you in their clothes, shoes, face, body. Be, for just a moment that complete and total stranger. Experience the full force of real compassion.

But lets not stare, folks, that just creeps people out, no matter how much you love them.

Our connection to one another is the most valuable possession we have. It is what keeps the world spinning. Our diversity keeps it interesting. Loving one another, even if from a distance, is what will heal us all. But, hey, you don't have to take my word on it. But maybe you should at least listen to His Holiness, The Dalai Lama, spiritual leader of all Tibetan Buddhists. Maybe he's got it right.

You think?

9

Most days I would personify Life as a classy, brassy dame: sharply kind and darkly beautiful with a great sense of the absurd. Other days, I would have to say that Life is more like a slightly demented, hot-flash riddled hooker with an eye twitch, a stutter and a death grip on Barry Bonds' lucky bat. You have two guesses who is the ball—and the first one doesn't count.

He-e-y, batter, batter. Suh-wing, batter.

There are few things you can count on in this game of life, and one of them is the cold, hard fact that sooner or later you *will* take it in the gut. Big or small, there's no telling, but you can be assured that you will one day find yourself on the dirty end of the stick, brought down to your knees with absolutely no idea what it is that you should do or feel. Generally your first instinct is to curl up into a ball and simply cry. I think it's a good one. Why we as a culture don't encourage this is beyond me.

Sometimes reverting to an elemental response like crying is the healthiest way to deal with your emotional conundrum. Crying is a release valve of sorts. And if we stuff dirty socks into this emotional pipe to avoid the steam, it will surely, eventually, explode. When you come to this dark crossroad, it behooves you to let 'em rip. Sob. Cry. Wail. It is far better to let it out in a natural way than to let it leak out another.

There is no eternal wisdom in refusing to cry. Being a 'grown-up' does not negate its validity. You do not have to 'suck it up' at first blow and bounce immediately back. Taking the time to fully experience your hurt will help you to wash away the shock of it so that you can, eventually, drive on.

When you feel that urge to curl up into a ball, do so. Come into a Child's pose, a restorative yoga pose that literally wraps you up around yourself and hides your face from the world. On your knees, with your bum resting on your heels, lay your belly down on (or between) your thighs. Stretch your arms by your sides and wrap your hands gently around your heels. Let your face fall to the floor, resting your forehead or cheek upon the earth.

When you rest in Child's pose like this, you cocoon your body around your heart. You allow it to storm in absolute privacy, cradled away from exposure. Your soft underbelly is hidden away. Here, the most delicate parts of yourself can fully express their confusion, despair or upset. For this brief time you are safe to feel whatever it is that needs to be felt. And you offer only the strong line of your back to the world.

When you find yourself this low, wracked with tears and hurt, remember: It will be alright. While the heart may be too soft at times, the back is generally sturdy. You can carry more of life's crap upon it than you ever dreamed. Suffering is inevitable. But we all have backbones that are made to be resilient. Please, cry and hurt and curl up like a baby when that is what needs to be done. But always know that your back is strong and so are you. The storm will pass. It has to.
In all of our hearts lives the child we once were. That is at once our vulnerability and our strength. To understand that is to open the door to Life—whatever face she may wear. Most days you win. Other days, well…

At least you know you are alive.

10

No matter how aged or wise one becomes, failure still has the ability to whack you over the head with a baseball bat. Even those of us who practice equanimity can still find extreme disappointment and dejection over a failure. But, despite that, never ever ever, have I bought into the 'Failure Is Not An Option' cultural marketing stratagem. Puh-lease. Failure is always an option. And, if you think about it, sometimes failure is the *only* option--if not the best. Even if it stings like the very devil.

Just take a moment now, and stick your tongue in the cavity of your personal failures. Without painting those memories with the brush of fantasy, turn those failures into successes. Think about where you would be had those attempts not been re-evaluated, discarded or shelved. Don't pretend, be real. Odds are, you are in the place you should be because of those 'failures'. We are all where we need to be, and we are there as often as not due to the hands of failure as those of success.

From this perspective, you have probably never truly, abjectly failed. Even those really bad decisions, the ones that led to disappointment and/or defeat had some value over the course of your life. If we never failed, we would never learn; our experience would be sadly limited to happy, happy la-la land. And what good does that really do you? Erasing failure from your life eliminates a whole realm of creative possibility. It is not a simple, evil devil painted with a one-hued brush to be avoided at all cost.

So what, exactly, is failure? Failure means that your methods for achievement simply need to be re-evaluated. It is just calling for a little mental intuition and creativity. A time out, if you will, to re-strategize. And there is absolutely nothing there to be ashamed of. The best generals in the world all had to sit back and think now and again.

Failure is opportunity. It is reality looking you in the face with a little orange flag that waves you into the detour lane. And, I'll tell you true, most of my most fulfilling life experiences have come from traveling the back roads. A detour led me to yoga. A grand and expensive failure brought me to the place where I had this opportunity to write for all of you. And I do hate it when people give you the whole 'lemons-to-lemonade' schtick, but it is sickeningly true.

Personally, when life hands me lemons I skip the lemonade and give them back to the earth. They just might grow into fantastic trees. But, hey, that's me. I'm an optimist.

The challenge becomes mastering the ugly emotional response that arises in the face of failure. And that is really simply a matter of surrender and trust. You have to give over your perfect idea and realize that it might not have been meant to manifest in the form you intended. That can be sad, and you should allow it to be sad. But you should never let it swallow you, or convince you that you aren't worthy of happiness. You are. But maybe that happiness will come from another direction or in a foreign shape. So you have to be open and willing to receive whatever the Universe has for you. Take your failures with grace because odds are, if you really want something, it will come to you in its own way.

Whoever decided that failure is not an option should be bopped upside the head. Failure is a beautiful option that frees you from your ego long enough to show you what you are really made of….
…beautiful possibility.

11

The end of every yoga class is dedicated to relaxation. And if your class isn't, you are so in the wrong place. This may be the most important part of your asana practice as it allows the whole body/mind to assimilate the changes effected in your systems. It also gives you a few precious moments to simply be still and quiet within the grand flow of existence.

Theoretically.

But sometimes it is quite apparent that while the body may relax, that noisome mind is still chugging away at a million miles an hour. I fancy that I can hear grocery lists being made, dinner menus being planned, or chequebooks being balanced. And, at other times, I can all but feel that one student whose mind is busily sorting out some major issue that is clouding their life at the moment. It is a palpable cloud in the room, a thunderhead darkening the clear sky. In an effort to soothe these thoughts—from petty to serious-- I often offer this reflection:
All is well. All will continue to be well. Everything is perfect just as it is. It is completely safe to rest and relax and trust that the Universe is unfolding precisely as it should.

It works. If you let it. In the class and out of it, this simple affirmation is immensely liberating. It removes some of the larger burdens of life and lays them squarely at the feet of a higher power. You are not responsible for the crafting of the Universe. Your life does not have to be managed every millisecond of every day. Sometimes we just have to give it over. Otherwise we unproductively waste time lamenting that which is beyond our control, swimming furiously against a stronger current. You just can't live this way.

Believing that all is as it should be allows one to come to the resolution that life is not a bowl of cherries. It is not supposed to be a bowl of cherries. And when those cherries invariably turn into sour lemons, one can accept that without bitterness. Believing that all is continually well creates a perspective of equanimity that allows one to navigate the ups and downs of life without the emotional highs and lows.

This attitude is usually challenged by those who can't reconcile with the fact that bad things can and will happen to good people. Bad things happen randomly all the time and it is very easy to believe that they have no positive value. Disasters, accidents, random acts of violence all inspire this feeling within us. Why did Katrina need to happen? In what way is this horrific event positive? I can't tell you that. The positive results of this event have yet to unfold. But they will—they must. For all we know the Universe has a grand plan for New Orleans and all those who suffered within it. The difference is perspective. The benefits of such a disaster may take a lifetime to unfold. But it is up to you whether that lifetime is spent in negative reflection or positive momentum.

Our lives are but a blip in the Universe's timeline. And it is arrogance in the extreme to believe that it owes us a happy, happy, joy, joy experience every instant that we travel within it. It is our perspective that creates happiness and joy, our belief that all is as it should be no matter how bad it may be. As long as you wake up on the right side of the grass, your life is full of positive potential.

So rest for a moment and relax. Breathe. It will all work out just fine.

12

I find that I must make a confession: I have absolutely nothing for you at this moment. No words of wisdom. No ideas about the nature of life and living. Not even anything interesting to say about one of my great loves, yoga. Perhaps it is the head cold. Perhaps it is just a case of the summertime lazies, I surely don't know. But what I do know is that my creative juices feel about as dried up as Lake Okeechobee in March.
I have decided not to let it upset me. This is just the nature of things: Some days you've got it, some days you don't. Right now, I don't got it. I got nothing. And that's okay.

Like a wheel, one's life goes up and down. Sometimes that cycle is daily, sometimes weekly, sometimes it shows little rhythm at all. But you can certainly count on it to show you high points of brilliance with an equal measure of stunning dullness. Nobody is Einstein all the days of their life—not even Einstein himself. As a genius, I'm sure he recognized this and let the field of his mind lay fallow for a bit, perhaps abandoning the chalkboard for times to do absolutely nothing.

Yet, even being aware of this, I find all too often that the concept of doing nothing is a particularly difficult one for people to swallow. Somehow we must have the answers all the time. We must have something to do all of the time. Just sitting still and experiencing that strange space of nothingness, makes most people twitch. Idle hands are the Devil's workshop, don't you know. (No, I don't, thank you very much.)

This act of doing nothing can be extremely valuable. Just think of all the times you took action when you shouldn't have and just made things worse. Or when you voiced an opinion that you weren't entirely sure of and found yourself in hot water. The practice of doing nothing or saying nothing could have benefited you had you only allowed it to be of value. The belief that something is always better than nothing is a fallacy. Nothing is worthy all on its own and nothing to be afraid of. Perhaps this aversion to nothingness is why many people have such a hard time practicing meditation. It is an exercise in courting nothingness. Just sit still, breathe and be present. That's right. Do nothing. Say nothing. Think nothing. Just be.

What happens when we accept nothingness is that we find everything. We find a remarkable freedom and a surprising expansiveness. The Universe sprang from nothingness and can be experienced within that same field of emptiness. If you allow yourself to be still and open to the opportunities of doing nothing, you may just discover the richness of that particular 'empty' space. Cultivating the art of nothingness allows one to slow down and recognize the vivid contrast between something for something's sake and an action, thought or deed that really matters. If you've never accepted the value of nothing, then you can't really know what is the right something. It dispels illusion. It is part of the unique balancing act that is a healthy life.

Repeat after me, "It's okay not to have all the answers all the time. It's perfectly fine to do nothing or say nothing when I don't know what to do or say. I will accept the moments of idle nothingness as an opportunity to be." Good. Now go watch the waves roll in. Get lost in the clouds—literally. Take this opportunity to use nothing for your greatest benefit.

I just did.

13

It is remarkably easy to stay busy. In this era of cell phones and television, multi-tasking and appointment setting, it is not difficult at all to find our days crammed to the brink with things that must get done. And it seems that for every second of every day there is someone, somewhere, telling us that we could be doing more. We often oblige, packing one more task into the day regardless of how it affects us. We simply accept the premise that doing is being. And if, heaven forbid, we stop doing, we cease being valuable. Any number of health problems can be assigned to this kind of thinking. We've even named it: Stress. Yet still we simply shrug and sigh. "Oh, well, that's life. I'll relax when I can find the time."

No, no, no. Relaxing is not something one tasks. Relaxation is a state of mind. This is a hard lesson for many Westerners to swallow, and one reason, I believe, that yoga often finds itself dismissed.

The practice of yoga demands that, at the very least, for one and a half hours a week you let go of all the things that identify you. That you abandon that which allows your mind—and your life—to remain incessantly busy. The mind attaches itself to these things. It adores being busy because then it doesn't have to think. It doesn't have to spend any time with itself or the "real questions." Now maybe that sounds odd. How can the mind be working but not thinking? Well, take 10 minutes and put that theory to the test. Set a timer, turn off the cell, unplug the phone. Cover the TV with a sheet. Sit in a room completely alone and try to separate your awareness from your thoughts. I know, easier said than done, but try. For me.

What you will find is a constant barrage of chatter coming from your mind. With nothing to keep it occupied, it will run around like a pack of monkeys let loose in a Kmart. It will jump from "I gotta do" to "I need to go" to "I should've ...". Your mind will make never-ending grocery lists of things to do. But never once will it really settle or relax. Nor will it ask the Self, "Am I happy?" "Who am I?" "Why am I here?" Now that's thinking, and thinking takes discipline. Why would a busy mind want discipline when it can run around free and loose, wreaking havoc on the hapless individual?

It is not life that makes the mind busy; it is the mind that makes life busy. And it is this very busy-ness that creates the stress we all desperately try to ignore. Now, there is a solution, and you've probably already guessed what it is. Oh, yes, that's right: Yoga. More than just a series of exercises that allow the body to loosen and stretch, the simple practice of yoga can help organize the mind to distinguish between being and doing.

This thought shift inspires a calmness that lasts longer than the time you spend in class. Yoga will teach you the tools needed to tame the "monkey-mind" and set about finding more relaxed and focused days. And, when that happens, those external voices screaming about the value of busy-ness sound just like what they are: ridiculous monkeys beating the drum of nonsense. You are not what you do. You are what you are, and no amount of running around can change it.

So make some peace with that. Because relaxation is just a state of mind.

There is a bedrock concept in yoga that Spock would call "illogical". But the great lesson within it is that it doesn't have to be logical. Reasonable or not, it simply is.

We call this *active surrender*. It is the point within a posture where you are fully engaged, but the tight reins of control have been released. You tap into experiential awareness, breaking the pose down to its most elemental presence. You are quite simply there. You've got it. You don't have to drive it. You can just feel and be and enjoy. When you reach that point of active surrender, the mind truly understands that there is nothing for it to do. There is nothing more to think about because you trust completely that you have come to where you need to be. The posture, then, becomes an experience of perfect stillness. Even if the legs are trembling and beads of sweat are rolling off your brow. The core of you is entirely still.

You are fully present and not thinking about it. It's a tough balance. Your mind is engaged enough to get you where you need to be: Shoulders open, spine long, focused breath. It is to help you determine if you are out of place: My knees hurt; My neck is crunched up. The mind helps sort out if you are resisting the posture anywhere: I'm clenching in the thighs. My jaw is locked. Release, relax. And that's it. It is not involved in continued interpretation, analyses or management. The wise mind is like really good jockey. Get 'er out of the gate and keep 'er on the course. Then shut up and ride. Trust that the work has been done and the self knows where it is going.

All too often the mind is incessantly engaged, convinced it must control all the minutiae. That still core gets bombarded with irrelevant mental dominance. Not just in yoga, but all of life. It prevents us from operating out of that still place where real understanding and experience live. But if you master the concept of active surrender, you begin to understand how to find that place at will. On or off the mat.

Because sometimes, the very best thing you can do is absolutely nothing at all. Sometimes you need to stand silently still and just be present where ever you are. If something needs to happen you should trust that it will. If it doesn't than it wasn't meant to be. Constantly pushing, scheming, managing will only make you tired. And busy. There comes a

point when it has all been reasoned out, it has all been set to motion, and you have to let go of it. You have to take the experience, take the ride and surrender yourself over.
Everything has its place. Everything has its part to play. The trick is in the discernment, the act of knowing when one aspect or another is meddling in things that are none of its affair. Logic and spirit speak different languages. You can speak with each of them, but rarely can they speak to each other. There is no point in letting one nag away at your experience while the other, as is its nature, sits still in the center.

The mind is an objective tool. It has great value and purpose. And one purpose is to take you to the appropriate point where you can move into the subjective experience. Where you can leave the mind at the gate and move on. You can then cross the border, so to say, into intuition, faith and patience knowing full well that all that has to be done has been done.

Then you will have met Active Surrender. An illogical and tricky bloke, but definitely one worth knowing.

15
Challenge is the fertilizer of life.

We all know what fertilizer is, right? And sometimes that is exactly what it feels like. Despite that, fertilizer is what makes things grow, just as challenge is what makes you grow. It is an inescapable fact of life.
In yoga we flirt with the edges of challenge, pushing our comfort zones right to the brink. To practice yoga is to push your limits of physical, mental and spiritual understanding. We ask our Selves to go boldly where they have never gone before, to seek out new life and new civilizations. (Oh, wait, that's something else…)

This expansion is not always pleasant. And, if practiced without awareness of our primary boundaries, it can be overwhelming. Discovering exactly where these original thresholds lie is a challenge unto itself. But it is critical—critical—that we know where we are: My body's limit is this; My mind understands this; My life is here. This is primary awareness. Once you have achieved primary awareness, it becomes time to push, ever so gently, out towards the unexplored. You may be pleasantly surprised by how much you have underestimated yourself. You may be shocked at your levels of resistance.

Enter Challenge. Challenge arrives when you least expect it, and usually when you're certain you don't want it. It could be your yoga instructor taking you somewhere you never thought to go. It could be a posture easily managed last week, but completely unmanageable today. It could be non-yoga entirely: a stolen car or phone call from the doctor. You never know what form challenge takes, be it delightful mulch or stinky manure, but, be assured, when it is time for you to grow challenge will be there.

The trick becomes to look challenge in the eye and say, "I accept." "I see you, Challenge. And I call." No matter how mundane or how esoteric, it behooves you to be aware that challenge has a valuable purpose. Within challenge lies lessons and opportunities. In them lie answers to unrealized questions or damaging patterns. This is an opportunity to expand your boundaries. Look deep and wake up. It's time to grow, little spirit, time to move on.

For beyond the face of challenge lies a bald truth: why? Why did this challenge choose me? Why did I choose it? A simple physical challenge could have an equally simple answer. Why can't I touch my toes in a forward fold? Because I sit in a chair all day. Because my lower back was injured in a car crash. There could be a hundred reasons, and by accepting the challenge and answering its inquiry, you now know something more about yourself. You have broken the surface and are now free to move beyond. For more intense challenges, life challenges, the answers may be a little uglier, a little more painful. But that only makes you more beautiful for accepting.

Looking within is the very first lesson yoga should teach you. And challenge is one tool to help you see what goes on inside your heart and spirit. What motivates you and what holds you back. If you never manage *Hanumanasana*, but learn to truly see yourself, than you can count yourself among the yogi. And if you can see a challenge for what it is, then you are marching down the right path.

So open up, everybody. Be bold. Be brave. Challenge has a gift for you. What is it?

The difference between a choice and a decision is about as large as the space between embracing bodies. But, given the nature of the quantum universe, this infinitesimal space is actually as large as a galaxy or two. Decisions and choices are the same leaf of paper in a book, capable of carrying the same tale or two different stories entirely.

Our lives are a series of choices. Every day, all the time, we are making choices. Do this or not. Buy this or that. Some choices are made without thinking. As a matter of fact, most of our choices are made by rote, either a reflection of our conditioning or whatever option is easiest and most familiar. We know what we know, we like what we like, and our daily choices most often demonstrate that.

I don't say that that is necessarily a bad thing. If we continually familiarize ourselves with good information, right thinking and conscious lifestyles, then our subconscious choices will usually be wise ones. But if we simply think as we are told, worship at the altar of Madison avenue, or believe that we really have 'no choice' than our choices choose for us and we often find ourselves in the wrong place. Learning to make smart choices is as easy as being informed and following the consequences of your choices through to their logical and natural conclusion. This is one of the many things I love about the study of yoga. It demonstrates in a visceral way how a simple choice, sometimes even an unconscious one, can have rippling effects. Like a cascade, yoga teaches you how your choices play out. This is a rare and blessed opportunity to see things all the way through to a possibly surprising outcome.

For instance, a simple choice in a balancing posture can lead to steadiness or disaster. An adjustment that may seem unrelated to the task at hand can lead you to great ease and confidence or send you tumbling ignominiously to your butt. I've been in both sets of shoes, and landing on your duff in a room full of people is not a choice I think any of us would make willingly.

So we become aware. If my knee rotates gently then my hip opens and relaxes. Ah, that's better. Now that my hip is open my foot feels wider and more steady. Ah, I feel more sturdy. Now that I feel more sturdy my jaw relaxes because I'm not concentrating so hard. Because my jaw is relaxed my neck softens and my shoulders can drop another inch or so. Ah, this pose is much easier now. Like a ripple effect, the simple choice of rotating the knee has created a better pose and a more positive experience. This is good. Not only for you, but for everybody that is around you. Your steadiness radiates through the room, perhaps helping others find their own. All of this comes from a small, simple, aware choice.

This type of choosing travels with you out into the world. Once you have discovered the ability to follow your choices through their entire course, you find that you almost always do it. And not just in matters that have to do with your yoga. From plastic bags, to incandescent bulbs, to beef, to air conditioning, to TV programming, your small choices have great effect on not only you and your life, but on all of our lives.

I can't tell you what choices are smart for you. I know what choices help create the world I want my family to enjoy—and I hope you can learn to do the same.

It all starts with a simple choice to make better choices. No big deal at all.

17

I find it disturbing when the citizens of the world's leading democracy fail to vote. Seriously. This is a basic right that people all over the world only dream about, and here we sit apathetic to our great fortune. It is a shame when this is a result of sheer laziness or ignorance. But it is a sin when it is neglected out of a sense of powerlessness. As in: "Nothing I vote for will be heard anyway, so why bother speaking up?"

No matter your political affiliation, you must admit that this is a rising sentiment. Many Americans feel that their opinions—their votes—are being ignored by those in power. But instead of firing up a revolution, most sit down and shut up to just ride out the tide. Perhaps it is the hope that we will land on a better beach than we left that keeps us quiet. Perhaps it is genuine fear found only in post 9/11 America. I don't know.

But I do know this: Whether or not you cast your ballots in the boxes, you do vote every single day of your life. Those little slips of green paper in your wallet are the most powerful ballots out there. Where you put them—where you spend them—constitutes your opinion. And, believe me, where the green ballots go, those in power will follow.

Our current government has taken an incarnation that most people alive today have never seen. The great social movement of the early twentieth century has all but been repealed. We are no longer dealing with a government for the people, but a government for the corporations. And if you see that, you can see how to get around it and make yourself heard. What matters to corporations? Money. What do you have? Money. Even if you only have a little bit of it, you still have it. And they want it. We have to demonstrate our wishes by taking our money away from those who do not represent our ideals. We have to change our spending habits to really vote.

Outraged by commercial farming and pesticides in your food? Don't buy commercially manufactured produce or meats. Shop local and organic every single time. Get your friends to do it. Talk about it in your community. Cast your green ballots in the organic box and watch the machine begin to turn in your direction.

Disgusted by big oil? Don't sit in your monster SUV and complain about it. Drive less. Carpool. Take the bus. Trade in your gas sucker for a hybrid, or pester GM to bring back the electric car. Put your money where your mouth is and watch the nearly desperate auto manufacturers turn their heads and listen.

Worried about the rising costs of healthcare? Don't wait for the government to handle it; they never will. Take care of yourself. Eat well. Exercise. Learn about additional healthcare solutions like yoga, massage, acupuncture, ayurveda, herbalism. Educate yourself about your health so that the trip to your doctor is a truly needed stop, not a knee jerk reaction. When the demand falls, so do the costs.

Terrified for the environment? Why wait for those in power to acknowledge the problem? Solve it yourself. Give up plastic. Walk where you can, or take a bike. Change your light bulbs. Open the windows and turn off the A/C. Every dollar not spent is one that the corporations want back. They will change to get it.

This is the new America. Don't wait to hope yourself heard the second Tuesday of November. Walk the walk by casting those little green ballots where you want to effect change. And then add insult to injury by showing up every single voting day as well.

Big problems are not somebody else's problem. We all must solve them—one dollar at a time.

The Mahatma Gandhi once said, "Even if whatever you do seems small, it is very important that you do it." Take a minute to ponder that. What does it mean to you?

To me, it means that we are not powerless. It means that we are all connected in a way that has the power to affect the world. Not everyone can be the president, or the leader of the United Nations. Not everyone can be Gandhi. And we don't need to be.

Each and every one of us has the unique ability to make our world a better place. By making only the smallest of adjustments. Making the smallest of sacrifices. Changing, if even minutely, the way we think of and perceive our position within the social order. You do not have to be powerful to effect powerful change. We, the little people, can change the course of human existence with the smallest acts of human cooperation. Now think on that.

Some of the most powerful creators in the world hail from the tiniest, most innocent of packages. Seeds, ideas, kindnesses, words, children. Each of these things, if ignored, can come to nothing. Alone, they are too small to be profound. Or are they?

One seed connected to the Earth can generate hundreds more, enough to feed a family. One idea connected to a strong enough voice can cause revolution. One kindness connected with love can change a life. One child connected to truth became Dr. Martin Luther King. Given the opportunity, something small and potentially insignificant can alter the very heart of life in this world.

This connection is within you. It surrounds you. It is you. Every small thing you do to help magnifies in the world into a powerful force. One small thing inspires another, and another, and then, next thing you know: freedom for an enslaved people, an end to hunger in Africa, no more energy crisis. It is possible if you believe it to be. It is possible if you participate. No matter how small your actions, it is very important that you contribute.

It is far, far too easy to believe that we can do nothing. That our lives are too small to affect the world. That we have no voice. That we are powerless in the face of monstrous corporations and big government. Calling for a social course change can feel like towing an ocean liner with a rowboat. But a thousand rowboats — now that's a different story. Real change starts in peace, at home, in your heart. It starts from the smallest of actions and the simplest of intentions.

Ride a bike. Plant a garden. Shop at the farmer's market. Turn your air-conditioning off and your fans on. Eat less meat. Take cloth bags to the grocery store. Pray. Help someone simply because they need it. Talk to a stranger. Be a friend. Share something even if it is only an idea. Send $5 to New Orleans. Live simply so that others may simply live.

Great, great things come from small packages. Even greater things come from small contributions. Add all the smalls together and you get something large. Huge, even. Something more powerful than the mountain of apathy that shadows us. If we all chose to do just one thing, the tide of our paradigms would shift. The human condition would shift with it.

Think I'm naive? Then let's all remember that Gandhi toppled an empire with salt.

19

The older I get, the more I realize that a happy and prosperous life comes from the ability to be both flexible and aware. Not unlike a good meal, a great friendship, or a successful marriage, a healthy life is full of myriad components which all shift and jive in the quest for equilibrium. Being flexible and attentive helps one ride these changing tides, mastering the art of life's ebb and flow.

Now, when we talk about ebb and flow, we are not talking about 'go with the flow'. That colloquialism refers to a simple attitude. Ebb and flow stretches out over the whole big picture of your life. It is part of the nature of your existence and refers to the greater energies that fuel its course. And your ability to guide them.

For instance, while there are a great many people who take to yoga like fish to water, practicing it diligently and faithfully their whole lives, there are an equal number of students who come to it for a while, love it, and then just fade out. Their energy for it is pronounced for a time, but then recedes until they have fallen from the practice altogether. Maybe something else takes its place. Maybe baby steps of inattention took it out of focus long enough to be lost. Who knows. But this is how ebb and flow works. Energy comes, energy goes. And while it cannot be completely controllable, it is manageable. You can, for the most part, decide how you want to ride the tide.

Since your life is full of so many independent pieces, it is only natural that your attention will shift between them. We are forever determining with small decisions what it is that is truly important. And while our interest may constantly wax and wane, it never really abandons that which we hold essentially dear. Our personal ebb and flow remains within the boundaries that we determine. And these boundaries are constantly in motion, being realigned as we introduce new interests into the mix.

This creates a tricky edge between surfing comfortably and getting inadvertently beached. Sometimes, we take on so many projects that we have to let a few of them tumble onshore. It is a wise person who can take a real mental inventory of their life and say, "Yep. That's the one. Sorry, bud, but you've gotta go." Conversely, it is very sad when a simple inability to manage our interests takes something enjoyable (and helpful) —say yoga—and tosses it out of reach. Without a healthy sense of balance and a mindset of right discretion, stuff like this will happen. You will forever be losing things. Think about it now. What activities have you loved and lost? Did you let them go, or did they slip away?

That devil, Time, takes a bad rap for our losses. But it's not really his fault. If we truly love something, if we respect it and want it to be a part of our lives, nothing can make us abandon it. We humans are stubborn that way. It is not a matter of time, but a matter of focus and flexibility. It is cultivating the ability to see when something in your life is being a time-hog and redirecting the flow in a more healthful and balanced way. If you never take stock of what you are putting energy into, you will never be in charge of how it is expended.

Of course things will always come and go. But it is the happy individual who knows when to steer and when to ride.

A girlfriend of mine always leaves me saying, "If I don't see you soon, the clock ate me."

It's a charming turn of phrase, and for her, accurate. But it always makes me want to rush into her house and office with a hammer and smash all of her clocks like some odd revolutionary liberator, unsatisfied until all vestiges of the oppressor have been destroyed. It's not my place, and I know it, but it chagrins me to see such a generous soul slaved to such an arbitrary device.

And she is not alone. Did you know that Americans work more hours per week than almost any other Industrial nation in the world? Welcome to the land of the free where we are leashed to our jobs by clocks, wireless devices and emotional obsession. It has gotten so expensive to live, and been hammered at us for so long, that most Americans believe they must work like slaves to capture the elusive Dream—without ever questioning what sacrifices that Dream demands from your Life.

Your time on earth is not infinite. Therefore it is extremely important to spread it around. Your time is more valuable than whatever your boss pays you for it. Your hours of unpaid time are the most precious and real. They are the ones that feed your essence, not just your belly. It is an old cliché, but an apt one: Nobody ever looked back on their deathbed and wished they had spent more time working.

The majority of us do make our basic livings tied to the clock. That is a situation that simply is. But how much of our identity we sacrifice to our livings is a situation that we create. The American dream may seem like the ideal of achievement and liberty, but the quest for it can create an existence of anxiety and servitude. To the clock, to the boss, to the company, to our mortgages, to our insurance companies, to the government, to the hundreds of little things that we 'need' to be 'successful' and happy. At what point do you simply say, "no, thanks," create your happiness from the little things, and start to buy back your time?

Yogi Bhajan says that most anxiety is a result of your sense of achievement and your sense of timing coming into conflict. What else is the chase of the Dream but believing that we have to have achieve X within timeframe Y? Whether that means seeing eighteen clients before four o'clock, or being a major executive by the time you reach thirty, attaching your sense of personal achievement—personal worth—to the American timeframe is asking for trouble.

Things happen when they happen. Sometimes things never happen at all. Pushing like a maniac to achieve something with no respect to the capriciousness of the Universe or to your own limitations is only going to make you unhappy. I have learned that God has his/her own watch and ultimately, no matter how hard one tries to make it otherwise, we all dance to his/her beat. So it is best just to take a big, deep breath, relax and try to find the groove.

Of course, yoga helps. A juicy fiction novel helps. Taking one day a week to turn everything off—cell phone, blackberry, computer, TV—helps. Dining with your friends and family helps. Looking around and being pleased with what you already have helps. The secret to living the dream is to allow it to happen as it will, making small, focused pushes now and again that jibe with the rhythm of your life.

You might find the type of success you always dreamed about. Or you might find another brand of it entirely. Either way, you take the teeth out of the clock.

I fear there are few things left in the American lifestyle that are inviolate. Times change, things change, cultures change, and most importantly, people change. What would have once been thought of as an untouchable ideal by our grandparents has been modernized and commercialized by our parents, then abandoned out of hand by ourselves.

This kind of erosion has left the door wide open for Madison Avenue to create an alternative ideal of what the American lifestyle ought to be. Personally, I think it is time to hit the breaks on that kind of subtle slide and say, "No, this portion of my life will not be manipulated."

So let us talk about one of the few American habits that is still sacred. It's hangin' on by a thread, but it still breathes and mutters with life. Let us talk about the Great American Summer Vacation.
Ahhhh....summer... vacation....Do you remember what that means? Or have you moved so far away from it that the thought is only nostalgia?

For some it is the same every year—off we go to Nantucket to rent our little beach cottage and relax. For others it varies—what do we want to do this year? And for a sad few, it is only a far off dream long since abandoned to childhood. But the idea of a few weeks off to do anything other that what we do every day still resonates strongly in the American psyche. I hope it stays that way.

I guess what I am doing here is encouraging you all to take some time off and take a true vacation. Give up the idea of Busch Gardens and Disney World; Do something you have never done before. There is an idea brewing in our collective minds—one planted there by the aforementioned Evil Empire—that claims all vacations are a pricey amalgamation of airfare, hotel, restaurants and entertainment. This may be starting to convince some of us that a vacation is an expensive one-track-idea. That the only brand of vacation fun is what we see in the media. But that is patently untrue.

Not all vacations require soup-to-nuts expense. Not all vacations are about lounging on your duff by a pool or beach. Not all vacations are about stuffing your face with over-priced food that your hips will regret later. Not all vacations are an obligatory visit to Grandma's house. This world is a big, beautiful place. This country is a big, beautiful place. This state is a big, beautiful place. And they all abound with interesting things to see and do and learn that don't cost an arm and a leg or involve Travelocity.

It is time to resurrect the old fashioned American summer vacation. Go camping across the nation—some campsites cost as little as $6 and really teach you what it means to look at the stars. Visit Washington, D.C.; The monuments and the Smithsonian are completely free and an enlightening testament to the American spirit. Take a motorcycle ride along the back coastal roads of Maine. See some 'little theatre' in a small town. Go to a yoga class in your former hometown regardless of the style. Eat in a foreign greasy spoon. Paddle a canoe along a strange and unknown river. Take the time to show your children the fields of Gettysburg. Visit the Statue of Liberty or walk Boston's Freedom trail. A vacation that isn't centered around being 'entertained' is incredibly nourishing to the soul. And much easier on the wallet.

If we refuse to let the Vacation be manipulated for a manufactured ideal then we can all afford to take one. Even if it is only for a few precious days.

And that, friends, is the true pursuit of life, liberty and happiness.

22

Your yoga mat is a strange and wondrous space.

A simple strip of sticky rubber, your yoga mat has the potential to become a sacred space. It is a home of sorts, grounding and liberating. It is a place of discovery. And, as such, you just never know what you are going to find. Or what is going to find you.

The practice of yoga asks you to move within, to wake up and see. Most of us were never asked to do that. We were taught to look outside, to seek external sources of happiness: money, lovers, status. We were told to make something valuable of ourselves in terms of social identity. We were not taught to make ourselves valuable to ourselves. But as we move into yoga, this is exactly what we are asked to do.

So, we put our feet on the mat, begin to truly breathe and move. We move the body, we move the breath, we move inside. And, for many of us, this is the first opportunity we get to understand what it is to be within. What it means to connect. This practice of yoga is an encounter with our subtle being, with our very lifeforce. We see that our existence is more than physical, that we live on many levels, and that we have the ability to work on these varied levels.

Wow. Big. Scary. Concept.

But, as we travel the byways our inner self, we may also find a few things we aren't really ready to look at. Resentments, fears, truths. These things have all stored themselves in the subtle bodies, tucking away into dark nooks and crannies of the English muffin that is our spiritual soul. And as we work through the postures and breaths of yoga, as we come to true awareness, sometimes these things just release. Sometimes they jump out of the bushes with a big old Boo!, and sometimes they leak out slowly like water from an old, cracked faucet. But it cannot be helped and it cannot be avoided. Nor should it be.

I have seen these releases come in all shapes and forms. They are all beautiful to behold. But the most common, and the most bewildering when experienced, is the spontaneous release of tears. There you are, in a simple squat when, boom, you are weeping with no explanation. You don't know whether you are sad, or happy, overwhelmed or awestruck.

It is the most curious of sensations. People tend to backpedal here, to try and pull themselves back. *What am I crying for? Quit being ridiculous! There's nothing to cry about.*

Oh. No, no. no. Maybe there isn't anything to cry about now. But maybe once upon a time there was. Maybe you stuffed something so far down that just now, it has managed to work itself out. How beautiful to be able to let that go. Or perhaps you have touched upon the great connection. Perhaps you have received a glimpse at the sublime, the beauty of life and living and god. Perhaps you have uncovered the well of joy that exists within all hearts. That, too, is worthy of tears. So let them flow. Its all good.

We are creatures of vast potential, complex and multi-layered. We are so unwilling to explore that. It is too big. Too scary. Too unknown. No wonder people weep. But to release is to discover. To learn. To live. To be.

All you have to do is step on the mat.

23

There is an interesting theological notion out there that claims sacrifice is good for the soul. In one way or another, in one translation or another, this thought makes its way into most of the world's major religions. Even in yoga, though it be not a faith, this concept appears. And I find that when an idea crosses inter-religious lines as extensively as does this one, it bears serious consideration.

Where we run into problems is in people's perception of what it means to 'sacrifice'. Somewhere along the way, our collective consciousness decided that all sacrifices were grand gestures that equaled martyrdom. If we weren't giving something to another that created personal suffering, then we weren't really 'sacrificing'. If you think about it, this definition of sacrifice has allowed us to practically abandon the concept altogether. In other words, 'If I have nothing so grand to give, I have nothing to sacrifice at all.'

That is very wrong thinking.

Sacrifice is simply the noble art of foregoing small comforts or conveniences so that others may thrive. If you need examples of this, simply look at Mother Theresa or Mahatma Gandhi. These two were Michelangelos of sacrifice, and they were the most joyous of people. Without a stitch of martyrdom between them, they made many small chips of sacrifice, whittling away at the marble of selfishness to find the beautiful *David* within. Sure, at times they probably found challenges, but they did not give away their lives, liberty or happiness. And still they managed to serve the greater good.

Sacrifice does not need to equal suffering. You can sacrifice any number of things quite easily and make a ferocious dent in world problems. You can sacrifice something small and simple to make a monumental change in your own, personal experience of happiness. You do not need to make a Christ-like offering of sacrifice to do good in the world.

Allow me to present a small example: Last Friday was a perfect, Florida day. Warm, sunny and breezy with a comfortable temperature of about 76 degrees. This was the kind of weather that we brag about, that we call to torture our Northern friends with, that hundreds of thousands of people fly hundreds of miles to experience. And yet, I was practically the only car on the road with my windows rolled down enjoying the air. I kid you not.

This means that almost all of the other cars had their windows up *and the air conditioning on.* What does any of this have to do with sacrifice, you say? Think about it. The average car loses roughly four miles per gallon of gas in fuel efficiency when the AC is on. That (for my car) is a little more than 2 gallons of gas per tank, per week. Do some very rough math here, and estimate if the entire population of Naples eschewed auto air-conditioning during our stretches of beautiful weather. That's about 600,000 gallons of gas saved per week, 2,400,000 gallons of gas per month. And that's just one mid-sized town. Take it out over the state, over half of the year when the weather is fair and you have just created a dent in the energy crisis. That is a lot of good for a very little effort.

And what did you sacrifice? Habit, comfort, convenience—in the realm of things, a very little personal sacrifice for a great big boon to the common good. Most of us can easily afford to make sacrifices like this in our lives. If we let go of some conveniences and change some basic living habits, we can create better health for ourselves and the world. Make the change in your mind and sacrifice becomes an everyday gift, not a once in a lifetime event.

This is the sacrifice that feeds the soul. Not just yours, but everybody's.

24

A friend of mine once asked me: Is it a form of violence to refuse the service of others? Not one of our lighter conversations, warranted. But an interesting thought nonetheless.

We are taught from a very young age to share. We are indoctrinated in the belief that it is holy to give. That charity is one of the finest virtues. We are rarely taught the value of receiving, or that there is virtue in a gracious acceptance of another's offering.

How many of you know someone who gives and gives and gives and never ever allows you to do anything for them? Don't pretend. We all know the selfless martyr. "Oh, don't worry about me. I'm happy just to do it." But is this really selflessness? Or is it just another, less jaded form of selfishness?

To do for others makes one feel good. It makes us feel valuable. In some instances, it makes us feel superior. Rarely is it a conscious decision of "I'm so much better than everyone else because I am so generous." But that feeling is there. To be selfless takes us closer to God—or at least that is what we are told. But we are also shown that it is alright to be satisfied by our generosity.

You must know what I mean. An example would be those people who donate a fortune to a charitable foundation and then plaster their name across the building. That is not selfless giving—that is a form of hubris. That is not true service. The instant that act of giving becomes qualified by pride, it is negated.

Service is giving without expectation of reward or recognition. Even private recognition. When done without pride, service is the ultimate expression of holy love. Even the simplest of acts can be divine if freely offered. This is giving.

But as all of life is an ebb and flow, a give and take, there can be no giving without receiving. To refuse to accept what another wants to offer is terrible selfishness—even if the thought of self never rises. To refuse to accept means that you are better than, or don't need, others. That you have more than enough love, happiness, charity to pass out freely without ever compromising your vast store of self.

What crap.

Even the strongest of warriors needs help sometimes. Even the holiest of men needs the support of others. The offerings of love, support, wisdom—even money—should not be turned down out of hand. Did you ever stop to think that the person offering wants to share of themselves with you? That they need to be of service as much as you do? That somewhere exists a cosmic balance sheet that needs to be reconciled?

One cannot give exclusively. Nor can one receive exclusively. A good life comes from a healthy balance between the two. If you accept that, you will find that you will always have what you need. When you are low, another will rise up to fill you. When you are full, undoubtedly someone will need of you. To give freely is divine. To receive freely is graciousness at its best.

So would I go as far as to say that it is violence to refuse service? Hmmm. Probably not. But I will say that it is a selfish outlook that does damage to others, yourself and cosmic equilibrium. No man is an island. And you are not the only human who feels a need to give.

So the next time someone offers you a gift of themselves just say, "Thank You." Even if you don't think you need it, maybe they do. And that, my friends, is true grace.

25

When I was much younger, I ran in a pack with a girl we nicknamed "Witless". Yes, Witless. As in 'Not-too-smart'. We called her this to her face. For our Senior week, the poor girl had to drink from a bright pink cup emblazoned with this rude moniker. (And for those of you thinking *how cruel*, be assured, the defamation was wholesale: mine was festooned with a big, red 'b' word.) However mean this may have been, it seemed—at the time—brutally true. It took Witless ages to reach a decision on anything and everything from lunch to college. To a pack of on-the-go teenagers, this was completely maddening. We probably loved her more for this irritating characteristic than we knew. Because, in spite of it, things always seemed to work out for her (and us) in one way or another.

I am so proud to still know her. She just finished a Masters degree in Applied Linguistics. Witless, indeed.

What I realize now—nearly 20 years later—is that she was never really witless. She was just unknowingly deliberate. She took her time. She did what needed to be done only when it was absolutely time for it to be done and no sooner. This is why things always seemed to work out. In today's rush-rush culture this is a rare gift. So rare that we took it for stupidity. And isn't that just a cryin' shame.

What she intuited (and I had to learn) is that things happen in a deliberate order and in their own time. Fruit does not fall off of trees with no roots. Babies don't materialize out of baking pans. First x must happen, then y, then z. This is how nature works. And, as much as we might wish it otherwise, human constructs work in exactly the same way. Life is hectic, busy, and hard. Sure. There is always something important to do and too little time to do it. Most of us develop the habit of just banging out whatever task is convenient to the moment, regardless of how far ahead of the line we jump. If we have a million things to do, how can it matter if we do #964,226 before #200,110?

Because without patient foundations of thought and deed, we will always be running helter-skelter, achieving only by haphazard. Because to accomplish only for the sake of checking something off your list is allowing yourself to live in a low-grade panic. All the time. Disregarding the natural order of things carries with it the very real possibility of creating more chaos, which then only perpetuates the sense of having too little time. To simply be more deliberate, and trust that there is an appropriate time to act that might not be this very moment, will help you find that calm center from which thoughtful, effective action flows.

As I age, I am learning this: Life exists in a strange space of opposites. It both passes quickly and ripens slowly. You can either spend your days desperately trying to keep pace, or you can sit in relative stillness and allow it to steep, acting only when the time is right. Only you can choose which side of the coin you want to live on. And only you can know when it is time for action. But if you are looking for peace, you must yield to the true nature of things and let them evolve. If you want the illusion of control, go ahead, rush away.

Me, I'm finished scurrying around. I'm taking a page from Witless' book even if it drives my family crazy the way she used to drive me crazy. Because that girl is a genius.

And she always has been.

When you utter the word guru, two things happen. People conjure up an image of an old Indian man in a loincloth, gray beard stretching down to his toes, and shudder, thinking you must be a cult-blinded fool. Or they conjure up an image of an old Indian man in a loincloth, gray beard stretching down to his toes, and think: "Hallelujah! A man with directions! Finally!"

These reactions are often the result of where a person is in their life, and cultural prejudices they carry around. For a yogi, the word guru comes with a lexicon of meaning. That meaning helps the relationship between student and guru to function. For a non-yogi, that word brings confusion—there is no meaning to determine the nature of this precious relationship. A relationship that can enlighten and enrich an entire lifetime.

The term guru can be loosely translated to mean "one who removes you from darkness" or "one who brings you to the light." When approached this way, the guru principle can take on a vibrant new meaning.
No longer is guru simply one who initiates another into the path of yoga, but one who brings another into a new mode of living. Just think, you, too, have had a guru. Who was the first person to bring you from the darkness and into the light?

Think back. Waaaaaay back. You can't even remember the first person that brought you to the light. Because the very first guru you ever had was Mom. She brought you from the darkness to the light—literally—and then continued to do so for many years. This is the first and most precious guru you ever had.

And I highly doubt that Mom has a long, gray beard, and if she's wearing a loincloth, well, let's not go there.

Gurus appear throughout your life whether you follow the path of yoga or not. People are designed to learn from other people, and every person who enriches you can be considered a guru of sorts. Eventually you may want to find a "distinguished guru," someone who moves on the path of enlightenment and has the ability to show you the way. Maybe you won't. But to dismiss the value of a guru simply because yoga isn't your bag is to deny the value of our very human process.

To question is human. And sometimes the questions grow so large that we do not have the ability to find the answers on our own. Enter the guru. This person will join your life when you need them most, and they might wear the most unusual faces.

My most personal guru laughs every time I call her such. A regular woman, struggling to find her own way, struggling to make ends meet, decided to try the path of yoga. As she struggled, as she learned, she shared. She taught me yoga, and led me from my darkness onto the path that I walk now.

No beard, no enlightened liturgy, definitely no loincloth. But she showed me how to think in a new way, and how to love the process of growth. She was who I needed at that moment in time to begin my own personal transformation.

Everybody needs a guru. And I think that everybody has one. Maybe two, maybe three. Maybe its time for a new one. There is no shame in needing a guru, be it through the path of yoga, or religion, or even friendship.

So keep your eyes open. Because when the student is ready, the guru will appear.

27

Non-violence has been a path of great victory for such notables as Mahatma Gandhi and Dr. Martin Luther King, Jr. They both claimed that it was the only path to a true, lasting peace. For yogis, non-violence is a cornerstone belief of the practice. It is the primary building block of the *Yamas* and *Niyamas*, or the rules of spiritual living. We call it *ahimsa,* and all other efforts are in it's service.

To practice ahimsa, one is asked to be non-violent in thought, speech and deed. No problem, right? How hard can it be? Don't take a baseball bat to someone's car. Don't smack your husband silly when he says something stupid. Don't zap your neighbour's dog with an electric cattle prod when they won't shut up at six a.m. Easy stuff…if you only observe it on the surface. However.

Is it violence when you grab that can of Raid and unload it on the roach in your cupboard? Is it violence to wear leather shoes or eat a steak? Is it violence to drive a huge SUV that gets 8 mpg? These kinds of questions are just the beginning of a huge canon of debatable issues. It is an endless rabbit hole with no clear bottom.

The issue of ahimsa gets even trickier when you move into the arena of non-violent speech. Again, it is quite easy on the surface: Don't scream obscenities at a rude stranger. Don't negatively reinforce your child. Don't tell lies for the sake of telling lies. But here we go again, diving down into the murky depths of the issue. Is it violence to tell a lie that does good when the truth will ultimately harm? Is it violence to tell a truth that hurts even though your intention is good? Oh, messy ahimsa! Messy!

And that's not even the worst of it. To fully practice ahimsa, one is expected to be non-violent in thought as well. This is where I always fall off the philosophical wagon and sit on the curb thinking, "Now that's just ridiculous." Thoughts are like hiccups—you never know where they come from or how to really control them. To expect yourself to be able to censor your thoughts before they arise is really too much to ask. How can one fully explore the depths of this practice if it is filled with so many booby traps?

The same way you handle everything else—one moment at a time. You just do the very best that you can and make choices that serve your own interpretation of what ahimsa means to you. When a violent thought arises, you push it to the side and say, "No. I will no longer think that." When violence is on the tip of your tongue, stop and think. Does this really need to be said and what will be the ultimate result? If it serves non-violence, then go ahead and speak. If it doesn't, hold your tongue and let the moment go by. Examine your actions and make decisions that help you practice ahisma. If something is too hard for you to manage, then it is a form of violence to yourself to force the issue. (With some notable exceptions like harmful addictions.)

In other words, be aware and be present with ahimsa. I still eat meat. I still kill roaches. These are my choices. I do not use plastic bags. And I drive a fuel efficient car. These are my services. Non-violence is a series of guideposts on the road to peace, not a corral for you to circle endlessly and then ultimately give up.

Just remember to be kind to yourself and to others. Then the rest of it will fall into place.

Over the course of my study I have had, naturally, many teachers. From parents to professors to yogis to colleagues, my course of instruction has been life-long and wonderfully varied. For this, I consider myself extremely lucky—variety is, after all, the spice of life.

But, invariably, where there is variety, there is also conflict. I have been offered differing perspectives—especially in yoga--about the 'best' way to perform and/or achieve. This can create confusion unless one can manage to integrate that conflicting information and make your own decisions about it. One must begin to make discerning choices based on intuition and intellect, rather than blind, following faith. We call this *right discrimination.* In yoga, and in life, this is a very valuable skill to cultivate. For instance, my very first teacher—and her teacher before her—commonly told students to simply hold a pose for as long as they can and then back down when they become uncomfortable. This is wise and patient advice. Sometimes a teacher will hold a pose too long for your body and abilities. Ignoring your own intuition about how long to remain in a position can cause injuries and create stress.

However, I had another teacher who was quite firm in his belief that you should hold a pose for as long as he instructed and not release a breath before his dictation. This is also wise advice. His point was that we are so ingrained in our habits of comfort that we are not accurate judges of our 'thresholds' and tend to give up before we must. In other words, how do you really know what you can achieve if you always collapse just as it gets difficult?

So, now we have conflict. Do you follow the gentle advice or the challenging? Who is right? Who is wrong? Well, to answer that I have just one more question: What day is it?

Neither of them are 100% right or wrong. And which path you take depends on a number of differing factors from the type of day you had to whether or not you worked out this morning to if you are getting sick, etc. You are the only one who can determine the right course for you and that course changes with the tides. Recognizing this is the first step to integrating your intuition and your intellect to come to a position of right discrimination.

If you were the whipping boy at work then I see no reason to push yourself beyond the boundaries of your comfort. Today. That might be a different story tomorrow when you are the golden child who can do no wrong. Then you might want to consider pushing your edge to see precisely how strong you can be. Ascertain where you are at the moment. Probe the reaches of your Self to determine what you really need to grow. Is it a tender touch? Or a thorough pruning? You have the answer. Its just buried beneath layers of habit. Digging through that is one of yoga's greatest challenges and one of its most precious rewards. If it helps, I also had another teacher (a little slip of a thing with a sweet honey voice and an Atilla-the-Hun like teaching style) who would always claim, "If you are struggling it is because you are in the place you need to be. You are working on what needs to be worked on—so push through!" I've always liked that advice because it prompts the right question. Why am I struggling? If you can answer that with frank honesty, you will always know which way to go.

Because being comfortable is not always right, nor is being right always comfortable. C'est la vie.

29

If you are anything like me, two days after Christmas the tree is down and at the curb. The house is fully divested of any and all pine needles, Christmas lights and décor. The presents are put away and finally, a huge sigh of relief has escaped your lips more than once this week.

And then it hits you. There's more? More parties to attend? More small talk to make? Torture, ya'll, torture. Aren't we done yet? But then again, maybe you are nothing like me and New Year's Eve is just a blissful continuation of this six week party.

Personally, I'd rather stick my head under a rock and cry. But then again, I am a creature of extremely moderate temperance and I just can't play that much. (Anymore…) I cannot hop around blissfully social from Thanksgiving to New Year. It makes me feel as if my scales are out of balance. My dedicated practice of moderation keeps me from tumbling merrily into the common holiday experience.

Whether you agree or not, I have to tell you that I believe this to be a good thing. Life in moderation opens the door to both longevity and happiness. With moderation you can enjoy all of life without falling victim to its excesses. As often as not, a taste will do you as good—if not better—than a huge, gulping bite. Heaven knows it digests better. Excess is a sweet little worm that seems harmless enough. What's wrong with a little fun, right? Nothing at all. However, it is the lot of fun that convinces you it is not such a bad idea to keep coming back that presents the problem. Excess makes itself at home as an invited guest and then can quickly take over, becoming master. It behooves you to think a bit before you allow it in. More people have died from pleasure than have ever died from pain. It's a scary concept, but true: alcoholics, drug addicts, chronic overeaters, drunk drivers. These people all suffered from excess and as a result lost their ability to see life clearly. With that ability gone they fell prey to disease, disaster or death.

Moderate, people, moderate. Life is best enjoyed as a variety of small bites.

It is easy to fall into the trap of believing that excess is only the process of doing too much. Excess can also easily become the act of extreme restriction. We may have six weeks of partying behind us, but I know most of you are staring six weeks of penance in the face as well. January quickly becomes the month when most people decide they are going to give up something cold turkey or make a life change whole hog. By golly, you will lose that twenty pounds, you will quit smoking, you will exercise for an hour every single day. This is another form of excess. And it is why most New Year's Resolutions fail. As much as we want to believe that we can do it, this "Hoo-yah! Failure is not an option!" attitude rubs against most of our basic natures. We want to be happy and content. It is our natural state of being. Therefore, moving into this mode of restrictive excess goes against our most basic grain. Of course you should try to lose that twenty pounds, quit smoking, or start exercising. That is wise and healthy behaviour. But you should take your time, moderate. It will happen if you are kind to yourself and make appropriate restrictions and appropriate changes.

Moderation is the key to life. It is the key to sanity. It is the easiest and most natural thing in the world. You are the only one who can choose to let it go. So have a little fun. Have a little discipline.

And all will be well.

Allow me to pose a question: What have you done lately to care for yourself? And I mean really care for yourself—authentically.

That means that the answer cannot be, "I bought myself a new pair of shoes." The answer cannot be, "I went out for drinks after work," or "I took the afternoon off to see a movie." These are unauthentic means of distraction from your true needs. Caring for yourself does not mean taking time to hide out from living, or anesthetizing yourself with life-dulling activities or substances.

Our perspective on self-care is sadly skewed. We demonstrate how we care for ourselves by working sixty hour weeks and then stuffing our faces with junk while we have a cocktail to dull the day. We expect to stay fit while enjoying the convenience of drive thru everything. And heaven forfend we have a problem, surely a pill can save us. So, lets work like dogs to treat ourselves by eating badly, drinking lots, over-medicating and sitting on our butts. Good thinking, there.

True self- care is stupidly simple. You need adequate nourishment. You need exercise. You need some peace and quiet. You need time for greater reflection. You need friends, conversation and love. I'd say that about sums it up. Caring for the self is to give the body, mind, and spirit what it needs most--time and attention. How on earth did we get so stunningly far away from the basics?

I think part of the answer boils down to how far we have come from the simple days of survival. Once upon a time, knowing how to survive meant understanding how to plant and harvest, how to hunt and gather, how to protect the body from the elements. Surviving was a full time job—but it was one that allowed for self care. When we farmed for our sustenance, we did not grow Doritos. Our food was nourishing. We did not 'drive thru' the fields; we actually had to work them. Our work was exercise. Time spent hunting and gathering allowed the mind quiet time to reflect on nature and life. Working together to keep a community alive created friendships and loving relationships. The nature of our existence fulfilled our basic needs for care by default. We had not yet cluttered up our time with illusions of "relaxation".

But today, survival skills are a far cry from what they used to be. Knowing how to survive in modern America involves knowing how to navigate the job market, how to manage a stock portfolio, how to manipulate the Credit Monster. Surviving today means understanding how to make and manage money. And money has absolutely nothing to do with loving the greater Self—or the physical one. This task consumes our minds, it eats our time and leaves us empty. Because we are so consumed, we turn to things that are "convenient" even though they can lead us towards self-destruction. Our addiction to convenience has made true self care seem more difficult than it is.

True self care is stupidly simple. Why do so many still resist? Eat a banana and care for the self. Take a walk and care for the self. Be alone and find peace with yourself. Take a moment to think about God and nature and the Universe for no other reason than you can. Your self needs only the very basics to be healthy, happy and whole.

And if the alternative is illness, depression or death, what on earth are you waiting for? Quit pretending that you are immune and wake up! If you don't truly care for your Self neither will anybody else.

And isn't that a scary thought?

31

So. Say you're driving into town down US 41. About 200 yards ahead you see a big, messy accident. More than one car, glass everywhere, people starting to get out and assess the damage. Emergency services has just arrived on the scene: police, ambulance and fire. What do you do?

The way I see it, you have three clear choices. One, you can turn the wheel, change lanes and get off the highway. There are a number of different ways to get into town without being on 41. Two, you can keep driving, slow down and rubberneck, hitting the brakes like everybody else only when it begins to affect you directly. Or, three, you can believe that it will never affect you, maintain course and speed and smash your car into the pileup, joining the mess.

Let's call these possible decisions proactive, reactive and denial. Or, more directly, thoughtful, thoughtless, and stupid. Now, let's say that this isn't about an accident at all. Let's say that this is about your life. What do you want to be? Proactive, reactive or in denial?

Every situation provides an opportunity to be thoughtful and proactive. Even the ones that seem to suddenly slap you upside the head. If you look back far enough, you might see where even these 'surprise' events sent up a warning flare to let you know that a course change was warranted. And if you really examine it, you may find an army of people standing by the side of the road with bright orange flags shaking their heads at your obvious oblivion.

Unfortunately for us, we often don't take the time to heed the signs. Disaster is viewed as the sudden turn of a coin when in fact it is a slow roll. Not only that, it is a slow roll with a bullhorn attached, shouting all the time. You need to get ahead of it, not behind it, where you can manage its course and dictate how it will affect you. This is being proactive. Yoga is proactive. Conservationism is proactive. Healthy financial habits are proactive. But if you never get proactive, if you never do anything about your health, your earth, your life, you will always be either reacting to or denying the problems at hand. You will always be behind the curve, dealing with a mess.

Luckily for us, we don't have to sort out the signs all by ourselves. Like I said, there is an army of people out there with their orange flags, waving them for all they are worth. But you have to knock the stupor off of your eyelids and look. You have to be willing to listen. You have to be willing to take action. Otherwise you are just blindly steering your car into a bus.

Some of my favourite flag wavers are no-nonsense, cut-to-the-chase, ironically funny and painfully clear whistleblowers that creatively inform you about the course corrections at hand. They open your eyes—sometimes with toothpicks—so that you can see the signs and decide for yourself how to make the changes that take you, and everybody that you share your world with, into a better way of living.

Please, read Carla Mills' Smart Health Choices, and watch the film *Supersize Me*. You must see Al Gore's *An Inconvenient Truth*. Read Core Truths, and Fast Food Nation. Read anything, anything by Yogi Bhajan. There are a million ways to get where you are going without being part of the mess. And any one of these people will show you a little bit more about how to do it. All together, they might just take you off the highway forever.

Alright, I'm putting my little orange flag down now. Go get one of your own.

Sometimes, life is just patently unfair. We can all agree upon that. But when it comes to exploring the reason why that is, I have found there to be two very distinct schools of thought. There are those who believe that everything is coincidence and when bad things happen it is just a result of the chaotic nature of the universe. We will call this the "crap happens" theory.

Then there are those who believe that everything happens for a reason, and when bad things happen, they are a result of choices made at some point during the course of our experience. Lets dub this the "divine pattern" theory.

I, myself, prefer the latter as it allows more opportunity for thought and reflection. Although I will give points to the "crap" theory for its greatly relaxed attitude, it does tend to limit introspection, heading it right off at the pass.

This "divine pattern" method of thought travels along the lines of an old yogic philosophy gaining popularity (again) called Karma. In its most simplistic dress, karma boils down to the belief that what you do will come back to you. Do good things, good things happen. Do bad things, well, bad things happen. But this is just the barest expression of a serious idea that expands beyond the confines of human action.

Make for me the assumption that our souls are eternal. Just for the duration of this essay, for the length of this discussion, agree with me that our souls return to earth time and time again to experience life. I know that for some of you this is a broad jump—feel free to disagree after we have finished talking about Karma. Because without that foundation of reincarnation, karma can only go as far as the Golden Rule.

Now, being human, we all make mistakes. We make big ones, we make little ones. We wrong people and we are wronged. All of these actions leave little scars on our souls, little ruts of behaviour that we are more likely to fall back into. All of our lives are built on redressing these wrongs, on learning about our patterns and scars and overcoming them. This is how we move toward enlightenment, shedding the ugly parts of our humanity and becoming closer to a being that can join with god. Its heady work. And work that takes awareness of not only our actions, but our motivations behind these actions. Only then can we be free of them. Even if you dismiss this idea as preposterous; even if you never believe that the human soul can do, or would do, this, karma still has a lesson for you. It is one of perspective.

We, as humans, have a terrible habit of short-perspective. We see to our immediate needs, often ignoring that which is better in the long run. We assume we can just deal with it later and then are surprised when we have to. This tends to make us a bit of a reactionary species, even though we believe ourselves to be clever planners.

The addition of karma into our awareness widens our perspective. Immensely. It takes our view out over lifetimes, out of our own culture and time. It allows you to see just how large human existence is, and, conversely, just how small we are. And once this deflation of self-importance occurs, we become better able to heal, to learn, to share. We see where we carry scars and those that we inflict upon others.

Karma reveals the pattern of your life. It is a road map of your decisions and options. It is a great teacher to us all whether you believe in its roots or not. Because even if you only live this one lifetime, it can become the opportunity to express the very best of our nature.

Did you know that your Sciatic nerve is the longest nerve in your body? About the width of your thumb, this essential nerve runs from the root of your spine all the way down your leg and into your foot. This is the nerve that causes lots of trouble, creating that shooting pain in the leg referred to as "sciatica". One way or another, without attention, this problem will visit most of us at some point in our lives. Oh, joy.

In yoga circles, this nerve is called the "Life Nerve". Meaning that if this nerve begins to speak up in the language of pain, there is something in your life that needs to be addressed. And I don't just mean on the physical plane. The body is vitally connected to the human experience, just as the experience is held within the body. If this nerve starts complaining, it is critical that you examine the deeper reasons why.

Generally, the problem is one of grounding. Not unlike a complex electrical system, your body needs to be grounded in order to function properly. It must be rooted in the present. It must be connected to the earth in a manner that allows you to draw energy without shooting off into the stratosphere. Your creator has given you this ability by creating a channel that literally allows you to connect to the earth—to ground--with every step you take. This connection provides stabilizing energy that is sent up the body and into the chakra distribution center, more commonly called the central nervous system, to be dispersed. This channel is the life nerve.

If this channel is blocked, you are unable to draw upon this connection. You may feel out of sorts, confused, harried or stressed. You may feel like you have no support and are completely on your own. This is all untrue. You stand upon an endless supply of energy and support. If only you would allow yourself to access it as you were meant to do.

This is one of the reasons that yoga is practiced barefoot. The feet are not an ugly afterthought. They are your stabilizing force, your balance point, your very strike point to the earth. So what do we do? We put them in high heels, loafers and boots. We insulate our feet from the earth as if they weren't designed to carry us through life on their own. We cover our energy plug with rubber and then wonder why we feel so tired.

Perhaps if we think backwards for a moment and believe that the sciatic nerve begins in the foot and ends at the spine, the importance of the bare foot would come more clear. See it now. The feet are like roots, from which we drink energy and feed the rest of the body. What do you think would happen to a tree if you covered their root system? Why do you believe we are so very much different? Just because our roots are mobile doesn't change their function. Life comes from the earth and you have a natural means to access it. If you close off this life nerve channel then you really are on your own.

Best of luck with that. I don't envy you the task.

So, for the love of Pete, take off your shoes. Get out of your car. Walk barefoot in the grass. Walk barefoot in the house. Slip off those shoes at the desk and wiggle your toes, stretch out those poor dogs. All the energy you could possibly need lies not at your fingertips, but at the tips of your toes.

34

I will confess to owning a pair of Gypsy Feet.

Every time someone I admire moves, I want desperately to join them. I want to live all over the world, resting for brief increments at various sites of note. I want to live in London. I want to live in Charleston. I want to live in San Francisco or Rio de Janero. I want to let my feet have their freedom and move, move, move, never tied to one location, never staying long enough to root. I want it all so bad that my toes curl with envy and my tongue curdles with bitterness.

Did you hear all of that? Does the depth of that desire startle you? Or does it resonate on some strange level?

"I want, I want, I want." This is a litany that lives within all of us. Whether your desire is for change, like mine, or for stability, for money, for love, for anything, want is a deep-seated facet of our human nature. It is desire that drives us through our lives, causing us to seek out something other than what rests in our hands. And it is this very desire that is the root of all our unhappiness.

This thought is not a yogic principle alone. It appears, in some way, shape or form in most faiths. Desire, or longing, takes us away from the present and shifts our hearts onto a distant something. We cease to exist within ourselves and begin to live externally. We seek things beyond our hearts to make us feel fulfilled. "I want this" creates an empty space within. "I have this" prevents that space from forming. No hole, no unhappiness.

In grade school they taught us that you only need four things to survive. Food, water, shelter, clothing. Having lived a while, I will add to that: companionship, love, and understanding. Its pretty simple. So how did we get from there to a culture that thrives on desire alone? We are forever being told that we must want something in order to be something. That desire is the new American virtue. And I guess that makes unhappiness the new American standard.

Please. Challenge me on this. Prove to me that the new Porsche that costs more than my house will truly make you happy. Because I can swear to you that in a year you will want something else. Prove to me

that a new corporate job with a multi-zeroed salary will fill your heart with radiant love. Again, I will swear, in a year you will want a different one. Desire is not a virtue. Longing will not make you happy. There is nothing greater or more perfect than where you are at this moment in time. So be grateful. Don't shun what is for what could be.
Even if you are busted broke, sitting on a park bench with a cup in your hand, you have something. You can find gratitude for something. Maybe you have a friend. Maybe you have comfortable shoes. Maybe you just have hope. Want whatever it is, however humble it may be, and you will find peace. Because you already have it and therefore you don't long for it. No hole, no unhappiness.

Want is a powerful thing. It is a squirrely, snakey devil that will never quite die. There will always be something to desire. But identifying this for what it is can make life so much simpler. Wanting what you have allows one to exist within fulfillment. It is to quit chasing after something in the ethereal distance and to simply rest. Take a moment to think about that. Think about the blessings that you already own, be they material or spiritual. I think you may find that you already have everything that you need.

So stop running, for goodness' sake. Live in the simple joys of a shared meal, a solid roof, comfortable shoes. Enjoy the people in your life — the ones that are already there. Love the job you are in. Adore the car you already drive. Be grateful for where you are because, for certain, somebody out there wants it. Just the way you have it.

So what do I have? I have roots. And they are beautiful.

The following is from a lecture given by Yogi Bhajan, the father of Kundalini yoga in the West, from July 19, 1975.

"This human body is the net earning of the entire spirituality, the longing of the individual soul towards this path of God. Now, we could say that through the grace of Guru, you have done bhakti (devotion), and the result was a human body. The human body is not just an ordinary state of consciousness. It is the ultimate state of consciousness, in gain. Gain! The total projected evolutionary system through which this soul can travel can only end up in gaining a human body. Human body gain is the ultimate stage of reality."

In other words, somewhere along the line, by being a good spirit, you have earned this body that you now walk around in. You *earned* it! I think that is a great spin of perspective. Why? Because I don't think that many people think about their bodies as anything other than their bodies. I have a body, big deal. Everybody else I know has a body, too. Most people don't make the distinction between the spirit as the guide and the body as the tool.

Through this organic machine known as the body, we, the spirit, experience life. We the spirit have earned the right to walk the earth in a human body. If we don't give thought to that, if we are not aware of the spirit within, we are simply flesh lumbering through life without a clue to our nature. If we do not care for our organic machines as if they are that divine gift, we are showing an immense disrespect to our Selves and our continued evolution.

There is an order of Buddhist monks who dedicate their lives to this. Avatara yoga is a practice that seeks to fully care for the physical body out of reverence. All of their actions are dedicated to loving and caring for the body: oiling the skin, smoothing the soles of the feet, eating wholesomely, performing yoga asana, meditating, breathing, cleansing the glandular system, practicing mental techniques to preserve the beauty and health of their human body.

Their belief is that "there is no flower, beast or star as beautiful as the human body".

Unlike the Western perception of beauty, this thinking is not steered towards a common 'ideal'. Each person's body is uniquely beautiful and their efforts to preserve this individual beauty come not from vanity, or fear of aging and dying, but out of a genuine understanding and reverence. The body is the vessel. It is a gift of god—an earned gift. And caring for it is not a chore, but a welcome opportunity to come closer to their true nature and forge the link to the Universal Consciousness. No action goes against this understanding. My guess is that they are pretty darned content people.

I am certainly not suggesting that you go whole hog into Avatara behaviour. But I do hope that knowing about this will help you decide to enjoy caring for yourself. Don't complain when you go to the gym. Don't wish you had French fries when you eat a salad. Realize that you earned this skin you wear and treat it's care with joy. Things that are perceived as earned are of more value to us, it is part of our human nature. Things that come cheaply are often treated cheaply.

So if your spirit put in all that work for this body, why would you treat it like a sofa lifted from the side of the road? You earned it. Now keep earning it, every single day.

It has been said that it is age that introduces you to your vanity. Hm. How embarrassingly true.

This particular demon, vanity, is the one who looks back at you in the mirror and prompts your usually worthy hands to pick and prod at the inevitable evidence of your passing life. It pulls at your skin, sweeping it away from the lower reaches of your face to remind you just how you once used to look and how far from your youth you have come. Maybe, just maybe, you think, a good moisturizer, a good sunscreen, or a good peel will restore that lost glory. Maybe, just maybe, it is time to cave in and go visit the plastic surgeon.

I catch myself doing this periodically. Then, thank god, I come to my senses and realize: I don't want to be twenty again. I wouldn't relive twenty-five if you paid me. Despite the loss of my once firm skin, belly, and breast, I really enjoy where I am right now. I earned every burgeoning line through laughter, sorrow and experience. I have tuned my face to the sun for the sheer joy of feeling it kiss me there. I have given of my beauty to my daughter, and if because of that my body has a new softness to it, well, at least I can say I bought something wonderful for the world with it. I like to think that this is what it means to age with grace. At least that is my hope.

I know that I have much further to go. But I live amongst shining examples of aged beauty. One of the most stunning women I have ever met just passed at the ripe age of ninety. She wore her age with a joyful grace. Her beauty was of the self and it shone on her lined face. It rode the drapes of skin around her neck. The brightness of her eyes may have faded, and you could have played connect the dots on the back of her hands, but she was just the most beautiful person in her heart, both gracious and giving, and this translated to her face. She was a lady and a wise woman through and through and this is what kept her gorgeous.

Many, many people will never give themselves the opportunity to express this type of beauty. The identification of self is completely externalized and it is only through physical efforts that beauty and youth will be maintained. This kind of thinking robs an individual of the chance to make the true self beautiful. To bring the true self closer to the beautiful radiance of god. If we always live just on the outside, chasing something that has long since passed, how can we enjoy the moment? How can we begin to understand what it means to really be ourselves? If all of our efforts are turned to making our physical form culturally appealing, will we ever have the time to make our real selves beautiful? This is the real work of the human soul and it has absolutely nothing to do with how we look.

If you want to stay young and beautiful, forget the face lift and do something thoughtful for others. Sit down and meditate on one's true nature, and on the beautiful possibility of the human spirit. Come to the realization that this physical form will age and pass—that is the point, after all—but your eternal nature is what makes you who you are. It is only this true self that knows beauty and can reflect beauty. It cannot ever be bought, and will never be found in any unguent or treatment. It can, however, be earned.

With age. And how about that.

The term meditation is bandied about quite freely these days. As the link between the mind and body is more thoroughly explored, this ancient wisdom is deshrouded from the mystery of ages and brought into modern light. It has been examined and tested, and if our physicians aren't giving it a resounding hoorah, they are at least dubbing it 'can't hurt'.

But as meditation makes its transition into commonality, it is losing its truth. It is being interpreted. It is being molded. Meditation is being shaped into a pill that can easily be swallowed by 'can't hurt', and is being slowly defanged.

The process of meditation is quite simple. The act of meditation is remarkably difficult. And when we think we are meditating, most often we are not. Where do we go wrong? Honestly, most of us lose it from the start simply because we do not understand exactly what meditation is and why we do it.

Meditation is not a series of guided images that lead you down a path of peaceful visualization. That is guided imagery, a wonderful tool to relax the body and mind, but not meditation. In guided imagery you are thinking; your earthly mind is present and distracted by the images you are feeding it.

Meditation is not contemplation. Tools such as Zen koans (the posing of unanswerable questions, ie, What did your face look like before birth?) are used to prepare the self for mediation. But in contemplation, you are still thinking. The mind is active. Focused, which is a step in the right direction, but still active. This is not meditation.

Meditation, contrary to popular belief, is not the act of making the mind blank. In meditation, one wants to void the mind of cluttered thought, yes. We do not want to be distracted by the grocery list or chequebook balance. We want to make the monkey mind still—but not blank. The mind, like everything else in life, is full of what you put into it. If you spend hours making yourself blank, what good does that do for you? How does nothing help you become a more focused and peaceful person?

Quite simply, it does not. So what, then, is meditation? Meditation is the process of stilling and focusing the mind on higher vibration. Meditation is opening up to your Higher wisdom and allowing it to purge the mind of filth and fill it with purity. Meditation is turning on your Heavenly receiver and shutting down your Earthly transmitter. Meditation is learning to be with the Spirit in blissful silence.

This practice requires a one-pointed focus. An absolute dedication to finding the highest within and being there completely. The process of deep, rhythmic breathing brings the body and mind into a state of receptive relaxation. The addition of a phrase, word or term keeps the mind focused on its pure goal, the receiving of Godforce. Your mantra can be anything, anything at all. I like "Sat Nam", meaning "True Self". I know people who use "Jesus, our Saviour". I know people who prefer "Diana, Isis, Hecate". It does not matter the words, as long as they are aligned with higher beings worthy of faith. Because this is the point.

We meditate to bring ourselves out of the earthly muddle. We meditate to find our own personal path to the Higher source. Meditation is not a simple stress relief task. It is not something that can be prescribed for relaxation. Yes, it does these things, but to make it a psychological action is to miss the point.

To meditate is to transcend. It is to trust in that which is greater than you. Done right, it is a true path to lasting peace.

I opened up my mouth the other day and my grandmother's words flew out. Without thought or consideration, her tones and cadence marched from my tongue before I could consciously swallow them back. Imagine my surprise.

Now, grandma is a wise woman in her own way, but these words were hardly original pearls. And never mind that I was speaking to a two-year old who's grasp on this sort of wisdom is tenuous at best. But I said them, and, oddly enough, I meant them.

I looked right down into his cranky, baby's face and said, "Henry, Patience is a Virtue." Oh, jeez.

But as I laughed at myself, and this communicative folly, I couldn't help but to think that even though this phrase is older than dirt it still bears out. Patience *is* a virtue, whether we like to think of it in those terms, or not at all.

Our society is, as a general rule, not a patient one. We are not accustomed to waiting for things to ripen, or taking the long view. In America we are encouraged to feed our desires immediately instead of waiting to see if what we want is really what we need. This is a continuing effort on the part of consumerism. It is an effort that is slowly beating Patience down with a stick.

You know that a three minute meal is not necessarily a good one. And instant credit approval does not instantly improve your financial situation. There are a million things that we could have this instant that are simply no good. Yet somehow, we have chosen to forget that a quick fix is often a shoddy fix.

Things that enrich and nourish life tend to take their own sweet time. There is a reason that there is not a drive-thru love window. Or an instant yoga mix. Or the ready-made baby delivery kit. Most true things in life are worth savouring. You have to, by their very nature, be patient and wait. You have to let them develop and find joy in the development. If you can manage to make this consciousness shift from "give it to me now" to "lets see how this turns out", you will open up an entirely new perspective on living. Then it will not only be the big events in life that bring you joy, but all events in life. A patient stance often yields bigger rewards than immediate grasping. Because, think now, if you grab the first thing that conveniently comes along, what might you miss down the line? If you expect everything to happen *right now,* what happens to tomorrow?

Life is a process. A learning adventure. Its not about what you have done, but what you are doing. And, more importantly, how you are doing it. What a relief it would be to let things unfold as opposed to hurriedly unfolding them. Let some of that responsibility go. Enjoy the mystery. Things have a way of turning out exactly as they should if you quit trying to force them. Patience is a virtue because it broadens your perspective and allows you to breathe. Practicing patience teaches you when to act and when to rest. It prevents your immediate desires from spinning you around like a mad dervish, bringing in its wake a measure of peace and, in its own time, a length of prosperity.

Its okay to let go. The sky will not fall if you sit down to rest. Your life will not spin out of control if you take a minute to wait and see. And if you truly believe that it will, I think maybe you should listen to my grandma. Never underestimate the power of patience.

It can change your life.

39

I hesitate to write this. Not because it is controversial or earth shattering. But because I am about to hold somebody up as an example and I'm not entirely sure he would want to be idealized in this fashion. He's just not the kind of guy that would preen beneath such praise even though he well deserves it. As his teacher, I am just so proud of his accomplishments that I've decided—hesitant or not—to go ahead and tell you all this story. It is, quite simply, the perfect illustration to a necessary point.

About nine months ago, an older gentleman came to my studio. Older, hardly old, lets call it "of a certain age". He had back problems and was carrying just a little bit of extra weight—no more than any of us average joes. He was a runner, and had decided to add some yoga to help with his flexibility. Wise man.

As a teacher, leading him through his first class was an exercise in "dear lord, lets not hurt the man." Stiff. Struggling. Sweating. Not at all uncommon. But he was of an age, and in a physical place where many people would have considered the practice too difficult. Too much to manage. No fun at all. I've seen plenty of these people come and go; it is just the nature of teaching yoga. I wouldn't have judged him badly should he have never returned to my door.

But here is where he turns out to be a shining star. He came back. He kept coming back. He sweated and struggled his way through postures that I know had to be uncomfortable. I was forever reminding him to watch out for his back, to take it easy and to modify. And he always kept on the fine line of challenge, pushing just enough to make progress but never enough to hurt himself. The man is a Trojan. And he just never gave up.

You should see him today. I haven't thought about his back in months. He's lost thirty pounds. In class his postures are among the most beautiful of any of my students. If I had a hundred students just like him I would weep with the bliss of being a teacher. As it is, I have him (and others like him, I love you, too) and it is more than enough.

My point with this is that yoga can change your body—can change you—if you give it the time it needs. This transformation took nearly a

year. A year. And he comes more than once or twice a week. This student moved beyond the point where he just did a little yoga. This became a life routine for him that I doubt he will ever be able to fully abandon. But it took time and determination to reach that point.
New students always ask how often they should practice. I tell them at least twice a week and, should they comply, changes will be seen. Over time. But if you really want to transform, you need to integrate yoga into your life daily. Now, I didn't say you had to come to class daily, I said you have to bring yoga to your life daily. That could be a video, a book, a routine memorized from class, a sun salutation, a posture, a breath, a mantra, anything of yoga in your life once a day.

Forever.

That's right, forever. Because a more true adage was never spoken than this: Use it or lose it. If you persevere, you can achieve miracles. No matter your age, or health situation. But it has to be a decision that you make every day, without fail, for the rest of your life.

I've seen the miracle of yoga. I've lived it. So trust me when I tell you: Stay with it. Even when you hate it. Because it always loves you.

One thing I love about yoga is that it teaches you about how things work. Like a thinker of old, you are encouraged to explore your body and mind so that you can discover—for yourself—logic. It shows you how to think. Not what to think, but how to think—meaning that it demonstrates how to utilize thought to its fullest ability without stalling it along the way in a rut of 'accepted' answers. There are no absolute answers, just the logical progression of thought towards truth.

Achieving in asana is a matter of discovering the continuum of your body's movement within the posture. Even though a forward folding position appears to be about reaching down and grabbing the toes, it is really about following the progression of a dozen tiny movements that eventually take you to the right forward fold for you. Sit down on the inside of the buttocks. Lean the torso out over the legs. Relax the toes. Bear the weight of the legs on the center point of the heels. Press the hamstrings to the floor. Soften the thighs. Lengthen the seat by releasing the buttock. Inhale deeply to open the belly and ribcage. Pull the spine through the crown of the head. Drop the shoulder blades against the back. Reach out through the armpits. Let the arms float out over the legs to reach the toes. If you can. And, if you can't, well, then, obviously you aren't yet meant to.

That's a truth you are just going to have to live with.

This ability follows you off of the mat and often shows you things that sometimes you wished you didn't understand. Your thought process is forever altered and you begin to see things—behaviours—that were once shrouded in short-sightedness. We are not taught socially to follow the art of thought progression. We are often encouraged to stop thinking somewhere along the line so that we can swallow the party line. This method of lowest common denominator thinking does great things for corporate industry and politics, but great wrongs to the world at large. Ignorance can be bliss, but it certainly doesn't do you, or your community, any favours.

For instance. Bottled water is a huge industry. We are sold the idea of fresh, pure water in a convenient plastic bottle as a good idea and a marker of healthy progress. Okay, now they want you to stop thinking. Because if you followed the law of thought progression, you just might come to understand just how unhealthy an idea this really is. One—shipping large volumes of water away from its source will eventually alter the area's water table. Not good. Two—the creation and disposal of millions of plastic bottles uses tons of fossil fuels that we really can no longer afford. Not good. Three—the plastic bottle itself will leech toxins into the water that you allow into your system. Not good. But at $1.25 a bottle, this is a huge industry. You spend more on water than you do on gas. Buy a home water filter and a good travel cup ($29.95 + $5.95 + tax = $38.00) and you are done. But you have to follow the thought out to the end. You can't just stop at, "Bottled water taste good."

This can be applied to almost any of the 'convenience' options being sold to you almost every minute of every day. Prepackaged food. Plastic bags. SUVs. No effort diet solutions. Anything that tells you that you don't have to extend any effort of thought or deed deserves to be examined closely and subjected to the law of thought progression. Open the door and follow those ideas all the way to the real conclusion. Even if that conclusion means that you will have to give something up or do something for yourself.

Then we might really think about saving the world.

41

As level as I am, there are still a few Westernisms that make my head spin 'round and vile words issue from my mouth: The supreme belief that we own the road simply because our car is upon it. The irritating habit of commanding one to "relax" when they are on the fringe of losing it. And the annoying tendency to encourage one who is struggling with the phrase, "It's a question of mind over matter."

Oh, stuff it.

There is nothing I can do about selfish drivers. Being told to relax is irritating, but it can pull one back from the brink. But the mind over matter thing? You can keep that to yourself because while the sentiment is true, the usage is dangerously flawed.

Yes, the mind is a powerful tool. So powerful that it can, indeed, conquer the base physical. You can force the body into anything if your will is strong enough. You can also strap a couch to the roof of a Volkswagen bug. But that doesn't mean that you'll get where you're going unharmed. The body has limitations; it has boundaries that can and should be challenged. But only after you have thoroughly explored these boundaries and developed a healthy respect for why they exist. Someone with terrible neck problems should not invert themselves into Shoulderstand. It'll hurt. And it'll do more damage than good. But, hey, it's a question of mind over matter, right? Your supreme mind knows more than the base body, so why not push it into something that you want to do? Everybody else in class can do Shoulderstand, so just put the force of your mind behind it and, voila! Matter overcome.

Bad, bad idea. This is a foolish abuse of the mind's ability. This is a selfish illusion of our own capacity. Only a clear, balanced mind can discern what should and should not be overcome. And most of us (now don't get all riled up, here) do not have as absolute a control over our minds as we would like to believe.

The mind is painfully susceptible to illusion. It filters our experience through what we show it. For instance, if I spend the afternoon in a trashy romance novel, reading about the life of Mr. Super-perfect-sensitive-stud, my mind—even though it knows this to be fiction—cannot help but to be disappointed when Mr. Regular-burps-n-all comes home from work. I am experiencing a judgment of my husband through the false illusion I have cast over my mind.

Is this fair? Is this true? No. Its not. My husband is a prince, and I wouldn't trade him in for a romance character. But the mind cannot help being polluted by what it is fed. And this is not a mind that is worthy of matter control.

If you are constantly giving the mind images of the good life, you will invariably be saddened by your own state of affairs. If you are always listening to hate-rap music, you will eventually absorb that angry cynicism and it will colour your experience. We create illusion. We pollute the mind with falsehoods. Then we expect it to control everything with clear discernment. Hmm.

It takes a dedicated person to rectify this. It takes a concerted effort to purify the mind to a place where illusion holds no sway. It is a state that few people who live in the modern world manage to achieve. This muddy mind is no match to our 'mind over matter' principle, and cannot always be relied on for this task.

If it were, every last one of us would be bending spoons and levitating. We would have no physical ails and could live forever. So perhaps the charge is not mind over matter, but mind over mind. Clean it up and see. Maybe then I'll let that Westernism ride.

I talk about becoming aware all the time. As a matter of fact, I speak about it so often that I fear people will soon start rolling their eyes at me and mutter under their breath, "Here she goes again." But here I go again.

It is so important to become aware. But it is also important to understand that being aware has absolutely nothing to do with what you think you know. And, truthfully, the more you 'know', the easier it is to fall into the habits of the unaware. It's a strange little Catch-22, but an interesting thought.

In ancient times, knowledge was a pursuit in itself. One learned what one needed to know to survive one's station in life. One undertook further learning because it fed the mind and spirit, bringing you closer to a higher understanding. Those who studied learned how to think, not just how to know. This set them on their paths to awareness. Great philosophers and scientists came out of this tradition; We still study them today.

But I see a frightening trend in the culture which encourages us to simply stuff our heads with facts. We aren't encouraged to really think—there is simply too much to know. The more facts that we gather, the better 'informed' we are. And then, we are allowed to simply react by rote to the facts at hand. No thinking required.

In this age where information is God, is it possible that we are bombarding ourselves with too much information and actually making ourselves dumber? Do we really understand all that we purport to 'know'? And, does our information obsession really make us any happier or healthier?

For instance, I 'know' that germs are bad. They must be because everybody wants to sell me some form of anti-germ spray, creme or gel to kill 99.9% of them. Use this product and you will be healthier, right? All is well, don't you give it another thought. But if I'm not mistaken, we need to catch some of these germs or viruses to teach our immune systems how to fight them. If we kill them off all the time and never learn how to fight them on our own, then we need to continually use these sprays, crèmes and gels. That is not a good thing considering that these chemicals have a whole host of side effects that we know about but don't ever really want to think about. So. Are germs really bad? Can't you just wash your hands?

Facts are like information potatoes. A good foundation, but you can't live on them alone. You have to use them, not just consume them. This is what your mind is for. It is not just a piggy-bank repository of information. It is a very unique and special tool capable of inductive logic, deductive reason and astounding feats of intuition. But, like any other tool, it grows dull with disuse. If you leave it on the bottom of the pool of facts, it will rust terribly.

Then you are open to being sold your fear. Which believe me, you will buy. If you just react and never think, you are never, ever, ever, in control. If you teach your children to value 'just the facts, ma'am', what happens to *our* Newtons, *our* Einsteins, *our* Aristotles? What do we make of ourselves and our culture other than a batch of 'quick-fix' junkies? Just think. That's all. Most of us aren't actually suckers, we just don't think things through past the visible—and desired-- end. Being aware means examining all the angles, even those that are darned inconvenient and have nothing to do with the immediate you.

Engage your mind. Question everything. The next great Descartes is you.

43

I firmly believe that language is the most powerful tool in the human arsenal. Words can elevate or eviscerate more surely than any drug or weapon. Nowhere is this more evident than in the history of nations, where rhetoric has created and destroyed countless civilizations.

I find that there are more than a few magic words in the canon of human communication. (Sadly, "Abracadabra" is not one of them.) Regardless of language, certain words have the power to open doors to the heart which allow us to fully connect with our humanity. And the humanity of others. "Please", "love", "help", "beauty" and "gratitude" are just a few of the more obvious. When they are strung together into sentences, they rarely fail to move a person to action or emotion.

"Please help me." You are made of stone if you can ignore this heartfelt plea. " I love you", can raise consciousness. "You are beautiful", changes a person's aura and uplifts their spirit. "Thank you," transcends social boundaries. These simple phrases touch the very essence of who you are as a human. They speak to our similarities and our unity. To employ them freely helps one move above the pettiness of modern life and into the higher vibration. They are, very simply, tools of self-evolution.

But these words, as powerful as they are, are very safe to us. They do not ask us to step outside of our comfort zone to explore the highest realm of mind and self. They are as familiar to us as our mother's smile. There are other words, powerful words, that are largely ignored and often feared because of their foreign origin. But this is silly. 'Please' is still 'please' whether you vocalize *please* or *s'il vous plait.* God is still God whether you say Yahweh, Allah or *Dios.* It is not always the linguistic articulation that matters, but rather the vibratory intention beneath it.

Which is why the Western fear of mantras confuses me. We have no problem accepting other languages unless is has something to do with faith. Then all bets are off. But these words are merely tools, magic in the same manner as 'please'. They soothe the human experience in the same manner as 'thank you'. I recently heard them described as "perfect chords". But I prefer to think of them as grease on the tracks to Destination: Peace.

Whether you verbalize, "Sat Nam" or "Eternal True Identity" is honestly irrelevant. I think "Sat Nam" has a nicer rhythm. It is also the original incarnation of the intention and fits well on a breath. What's the point of messing with that? Fear? Comfort? Pooh. Get over it. (The French still call a t-shirt a *t-shirt.* And a more linguistically fussy people I have never met. So you can certainly eek out a "sat nam", right?)
So, let's all inhale sat; Exhale nam. And then keep going. Allow every inhale to mentally vibrate with 'sat' and every exhale to vibrate with 'nam'. This simple exercise clears the mind nicely because the vibratory intention behind those two foreign words is focusing on an awareness greater than your own. Not much can stand up to that—certainly not the annoying person in front of you hogging up the grocery aisle, or the jerk who believes the red light means 'go ahead, o special one, red doesn't mean stop for you'. Inhale sat; exhale nam, and those annoyances are but fleas on the back of a shaggy, cosmic dog because now your intentions are higher.

Give it a try. You'll be surprised. Words are your most powerful tools for healthy living no matter from what language they originate. Choose wisely. Speak to one another—and to yourself-- with the highest of good intentions and know real peace.

Those of you that come to yoga for the spiritual point of view may be a bit disappointed by the average American yoga class. The Plain Jane yoga found in clubhouses and gyms, practiced in an hour of physical asana with the briefest of relaxations. You may hear such phrases as "Connect with your breath", or "Open your heart", but you will not often hear talk of God or faith or the deeper mysteries. True chanting is minimized, and only the briefest of mantram make their appearances.

There is a reason for this. Modern yoga has opened itself up to the mainstream. And, in an effort to appeal to all and offend none, it has closeted off some of its deeper aspects in favor of a lighter touch. Some teachers find themselves wary of introducing such fathomless concepts in a venue where students are obviously disinterested. Is this good or bad? I can't really say. Only you can judge the level of spiritual connection that you require from a yoga practice. And only you can seek out the classes that fearlessly address the features of a truly deep and complete yoga practice.

I, personally, require this connection. I love the spirit of yoga and the words, sounds, and breath that take my practice beyond the realm of flexibility. I already know how to stand on my head, or touch my palms to the floor. I have achieved backbends and twists and can stand on one foot for an hour. That is not the point of my practice. I need to connect, to feel, to be one. To do this, I turn to Kundalini yoga.

So what is Kundalini yoga? Oh, I'm so glad you asked.

In the simplest terms, Kundalini yoga is a method of raising your spiritual energy, cleansing the organs and systems, and toning the nervous system through a series of proscribed exercises and breaths. From an outsiders view, it looks pretty silly with a lot of huffing and puffing, chanting, toning and flapping of the hands and arms. There are plenty of times I have caught myself wondering, "What (huff) am (puff) I (huff) doing (puff)?" But beyond that, the experience grounds and enlightens you. It opens you up to connect with yourself and your creative source.

The philosophy behind Kundalini is rooted in the very act of creation. Shiva and Shakti, the masculine and feminine forces, made life. From their timeless place, Shakti descends, growing denser and more manifest as she comes down to earth, forming ether, then air, fire, water, earth. The human body becomes a road map of her descent from the crown of the head, limitless perception, to the base of the spine, earthly manifestation, with everything in between. Shakti finally rests, curled around the base of the spine like a slumbering serpent. It is your task, as a seeker of spiritual enlightenment, to raise this energy up the spine to join Shakti with Shiva and thereby make communion with the boundless bounty of God. This is to what the practice of Kundalini yoga aspires.

It is a fantastic experience, but not one for the meek. This energy is powerful stuff, and, if raised without awareness, can leave you quite exposed and adrift. But, if practiced with reverence and attentiveness, it will make you feel more connected and alive than anything I have ever experienced. It is my favourite yoga style, bar none. But that's me. Kundalini isn't for everyone, and you'll either love it completely, or hate it with equal passion.

But anyone who looks to yoga for a spiritual experience owes it to themselves to at least give it a try once. Aren't you (huff) even a little (puff) bit curious?

45

I love my job. Because, really, what other profession requires you to sit still, thoughtful and relaxed during business hours? And then pays you for it?

Teaching and talking about yoga is just about the best job I have ever had. You cannot imagine the depths of my gratitude that I am able to do it. But it is not always comfortable.

The science of yoga deals with subject matters that are not always visible to the eye. It deals with energies, of the heavens and earth and body. They are real. They exist. And if you practice yoga—any yoga—eventually you will discover what we talk about when we use these words. But when you start talking about these things to the average Joe, the reaction is disheartening. One can find one's self at the other end of a doubtful and slightly pitying gaze as if you had decided to take off your pants and run up and down Fifth Avenue proclaiming the existence of extraterrestrials.

Just because you cannot see something with your eyes does not mean that it does not exist. The human eyes can't even discern the entire colour spectrum, so how can someone be so sure that 'seeing is believing'? So, here I go. No. I am not 'out there'. I still have my pants and my wits. These things are real and valuable and you need to know about them.

Lets talk a bit about the Human Chakra System. You can't see it and you can go your entire life without realizing it is there. But it affects you nonetheless. It dictates to the state of your physical and mental health. When the Chakra system is out of whack, so are you.

Chakras are wheels of transformational energy that exist within the body, stacked up along the length of the spine. There are seven of them, although some disciplines add an eighth. Running from the very root of your body up to the crown of your head, these energy centers are powerful places within that express the nature of god. They help you tap into the great connection, providing strength, support and balance. When all chakras are open and vibrating with health you are better able to experience your emotions without letting them bind you, see the truth in personal situations and make clearer decisions. You are in tune with the natures of life and the full possibilitiy of the human experience. Study of the chakras is an extensive task. It is far to deep for the space I have here. Most simply, it is an energy continuum traveling from the root of the spine—earth—to the crown of the head—divinity. Not unlike a tree trunk, the chakra system takes you up, providing earthly stability at the base and heavenly connection at the top. Each chakra has an element that helps you make relevant associations. As you travel up, the elements become less dense, so that by the time you reach the top you are physically unburdened and free to connect with higher vibrations.

Maps of the system are universally available. I recommend that everybody take the time to find one and to explore these places within the body. A block anywhere can cause untold, indescribable problems in either the physical body or the emotional one. Finding a way to release them will open you up, allowing the free flow of energy up and down the spine. This energy is as important to life as healthy foods. Without it, we are merely upright apes. I can't prove that to you with empirical evidence, but you'll just have to take my word on it.

So now I think I'll go wrap a turban around my head and cluck like a chicken on the front porch. We esoteric loonies like to do that, you know. (Kidding, y'all. I'm kidding…)

46

Aparigraha—(n.)the practice of greedlessness or non-grasping.

I have spoken loudly and often about wanting what you have and living moderately. So much so that some of you are already groaning, "Oh, no, not again.". But these are more than just ideas to me, they are the way of my life. Keep it simple whenever possible and let the rest go by.

Now, I respect that we all need some stuff and I don't suggest that you abandon the quest for it completely. It is foolish to believe that we can go about life without gathering a few necessary things. (Which begs the question, what is necessary?) I mean, nobody wants to go wandering around town in a loincloth, or live in a cave. But, on the other hand, you certainly don't need two walk-in closets full of clothes to protect yourself from the elements. Or a house large enough to accommodate a circus to keep you out of the rain. This is just common sense and good old-fashioned simplicity. But the practice of greedlessness is just a shade different. It refers not so much to simple moderation, but to our awareness of how one goes about acquiring the things that we truly need.

This natural process of acquisition is inherent to us all and encompasses everything from food, to clothes to shelter—even to opportunities. It is simply who we are. In our culture, we are taught the virtue of aggressively pursuing acquisitions. You don't get what you want by sitting around and waiting for it to happen, right? You have to just get out there and grab the bull by the horns, wrestle it to the ground and take what you want like a warrior of old. This is how empires are built. This is how you achieve the American dream. This is how you get ahead. The message is everywhere. Be aggressive. B-E- aggressive. Ugh. This is very unhealthy thinking.

Really. Do you truly want to run an empire? Or is the small nation of your happy hearth and home enough? Is your goal worth the effort of wrestling said bull to the ground? You know what they say…you mess with the bull, you get the horns. Who needs steak everyday, anyway? And what does it mean to 'get ahead'? Can anybody explain that satisfactorily? Get ahead of who? And why?

It is far healthier to be discerning and considerate in your quest for attainment. Take what is necessary with gratitude and no more. You can very easily become the person who allows good things to come to you without chasing them like a junkyard dog. Change your thinking. Change your intentions from, "I will hunt down my desires," to "I will allow my desires to find me". This simple transition of thought will adjust your frequency, alter your electro-magnetic field. You can become attractive to your desires and bring them to you. Aparigraha plays a huge part in this. If you give up greedy acquisition, you are already more than halfway there.

You might be surprised at how much this attitude will provide for you. The practice of aparigraha is tough, but not unforgiving. If you share, manage the size of your footprints, and realize that not everything that you want is what you need, aparigraha will sort itself out and bring you to harmony.

And a wealth of possibility to you.

When my father was a little boy he was taught this: If you are ever in any trouble, go and find an adult. Any adult. When I was a little girl, I was taught this: Don't ever, ever talk to strangers. If you are ever in any trouble go and find a policeman or a fireman. (This was obviously in the days when the police actually used their feet and not just their cars.) What a difference only thirty years can make. I wonder, what are they going to teach my daughter? Don't ever go outside because any number of horrible people might find you, so best just to trust no one?
Sad. Seriously scary sad.

On the other side of the equation lie abundant personal accounts that detail the incredible kindness of strangers. Stories of people who have reached out to offer comfort or aid to someone they didn't know. Stories of people who have sacrificed for others without the benefit of family ties or friendship. These kinds of truths abound, and yet we still exist in a state of perpetual red alert, waiting for the sky to fall. Why is that? Why are we choosing fear over faith? Why can't a distressed child run to the nearest adult and ask for help? I'd help and not harm. Wouldn't you?

But then I am a yogi and my perspective is that of a yogi. I live in a state of belief. I have a good heart, therefore I believe that you, too, have a good heart. I think most of us would rather solve a problem than leave it for someone else. I believe that most of us accept some form of god and live in a way that respects that. I try to be true to these beliefs and live in a state of aware trust, understanding that my animal intuition will tell me when to believe otherwise. It is a constant effort. But my yoga practice has taught me that beneath all of our differences, we are all made of the same god essence. Our source is exactly the same. You and I are one. Harm you, and harm myself.

But I also believe that without my yoga practice, without this constant effort, I could easily fall prey to the cynical fear that exists like a virus in our cultural collective. It is this fear that keeps us intently focused on the worst of what might happen as opposed to that which is likely to happen. It is this fear which isolates us in the sad bubble of "what if…". Smart odds are if your car breaks down that stranger would loan you a cell phone as opposed to hitting you over the head with a tire iron and stuffing you in their trunk. Life is not always an episode of CSI. And we cannot live as if it is.

Now think about it. More than half our fears will never manifest. Yes, there are boogey men in the night. But there are far, far more regular good old folks who mean you absolutely no harm whatsoever. Develop your intuition to differentiate between the two rather than automatically assuming the worst. If you do this, you can better discover the common thread which binds us all. You can exist in a state of unity with mankind and with godkind. The two are not so very far apart. As a matter of fact, they are precisely the same thing.

It is this state of unity to which all faiths aspire. But you have to put it into practice in order to achieve it. Be smart, be aware and have a little hope.

Life is much sweeter when you do.

At this moment, I think it is fairly safe to claim that thoughts of family are high up on your list. Be they positive ones, "I can't wait to see Uncle Julien at Christmas dinner; It's been too many years!" Be they negative ones, "Dear Lord, please don't stick me with Great-Aunt Tilly for the menorah lighting tonight; She smells of cabbage!" Whatever your thoughts may be, it is almost a guarantee that for this short season, they revolve around family.

I think it is also fairly safe to wager that, while you are busy thinking about your family, you are not at all thinking about the *nature* of family. You don't have any choice in the matter, right? Your family is your family for better or worse. You just get what you get by virtue or accident of your birth. The idea of family is simply—if you'll forgive the pun—written in blood.

Or is it?

For the longest time I remember being just a family of two. Me and mom. C'est tout. But, for as lonely as that sounds, I also remember being continually surrounded by an urban army of family. Thanksgivings and Easters were often boisterous celebrations of love and merriment with many, many 'aunts' and 'uncles' who bore me no blood relation at all. And I loved them no less for it. For without the obligation of relation, our relationships were pure. They were given freely from the heart. This, to me, has always been the true nature of family.

Because of this awakening, and despite being an only child, my family today is enormous. I have one mother, but two more mother figures, two fathers, seven sisters, three brothers, four brothers-in-law, three grandmothers, four aunts, seven uncles, five nephews (and a sixth on the way), one daughter and three furry children. (I used to have a tree, but we moved and he couldn't—sad.) That doesn't include those folks that I simply consider friends. This is my family. And it is my family because I accepted it as one.

The nature of family is unity, love and support. Freely given and freely taken without the slightest thought to reciprocation. Whether or not you share blood is wholly and completely irrelevant. Whether or not you even share a common *genus* is also irrelevant. If we want peace in the world, we need to start by redefining our conception of what it means to be family. Everything around you is part of your family.

If you don't believe me, stop for a moment and think of this: Trace life back over a long enough timeline, and we are all related. We all evolved from exactly the same place. Humans, animals, insects, plant life, bacteria, single celled organisms, we all emerged from the same puddle of primordial ooze. Take it back further and realize this: our planet, our solar system, our galaxy, our universe all emerged from a highly motivated atom of hydrogen. You can go back further if you want, into the reaches of cosmic consciousness. If you just stop for a moment and remove yourselves from the separatist concept of family as mine and theirs, you might discover that there is only One. We are a family of existence.

Let yourself be a part of it and take as much solace from Mother Nature's arms as from mother's. Let a cat provide sympathy when your heart hurts. Allow a blade of grass to educate you on the nature of truth. Offer up your own love and support to all things known and unknown, animal, vegetable and mineral. We will save the world by loving all of it as family—not just the pieces that are like you.
Blessed be, one and all. Namaste.

49

What kind of columnist would I be if I had a column on Thanksgiving and did not speak about gratitude? (An original one, I assume. But, hey, who am I to buck convention?)

Once a year we all gather together under the pretext of being "thankful." We eat an obscenely large dinner with family and friends and tell each other how grateful we are for one another. And then we go home, thankful again, when it is all over. I wonder, how true this gratitude is? Personally, I have never cared for this holiday. Its not my favorite kind of meal, and my family is so far flung that we just gather when we can. In addition, I have some lingering reservations about the truth of Thanksgiving. Enough that I don't feel comfortable sitting in a tableaux of Pilgrims and Indians knowing the sordid outcome of what happened after.

Despite this, I think it is fantastic that the idea of gratitude at least makes a guest appearance in the American diet. We tend to think of ourselves as naturally deserving and take things as they come to us without a second thought to our good fortune. This kind of thinking is a slippery slope towards disconnecting from each other and from the bounty of our generous earth. So I am willing to set my personal grievances aside and celebrate this holiday if for no other reason than it brings the word gratitude to the front of our minds if even for one small day.

But what would life be like if the practice of gratitude stepped away from the turkey and shouted out loud every day of the year? It is fairly easy to feel grateful when you are surrounding a bounteous feast with loved ones by your side. Can this kind of thanks live in the daily grind? It can. And it must.

It is on the days when your significant has said something particularly foul as you are rushing out the door 10 minutes late, and every stoplight catches you because some land yacht in the passing lane chooses to travel at a crisp 25 miles an hour in a 55 zone that you need to find gratitude. It is the day when your cell phone dies as your tire blows on the way to a critical, life-altering meeting and no one will stop to help you that you need to practice gratitude. It is when life sucks the most that you need to think of five things that you are grateful for. Right there. In the car. On the side of the road. In a nasty person's face.

Why?

Because this inspires a complete perspective change. If you can honestly find five things to be grateful for when the chips are down, you can change the way you look at the world. Gone will be the self-centered, entitled person and in its place will be someone who recognizes that life is full of gifts. Nobody owes you anything, and the instant you come to terms with that, everything lightens up.

Every moment is a gift. Even the bad ones. We are here to learn, and to understand one another. To live in gratitude is to live connected to the joys of life and to cultivate a sense of humour about its challenges.

This cannot happen just one day a year. Once a year is simply not enough. Hopefully, this year, you can all take Thanksgiving and tuck it into your pocket to carry like a talisman of hope and light. You can pull it out and hold it in your hands when times are tough. You can share it with others every day for the rest of your life. Gratitude is like love.

There is simply never too much.

50

As the busy season stares us in the face and our population inevitably swells, I thought it prudent to discuss something incredibly profound and idiotically simple.

You are not the only person on the face of the Earth. What you are doing is not the only thing happening in the universe. And that means you will just simply have to share.

I know, deep, right? But, hey, that's what I'm here for.

As a human being living a modern life, it is easy to forget that every last one of us is in the same boat. Regardless of social standing, education, career, ethnicity or age, we are all simply people trying to live a happy life. In general, we all have similar problems and similar desires. At some point in time everybody has experienced the depths of a broken heart or the joys of real love. We have all lost something dear to us and found something we never thought we were looking for. We are all just moving through life doing the very best that we can.

It is so easy to forget that when the process of living takes over the driver's wheel. Everyday tasks beat their drum until their rhythm becomes the only cadence you hear. I have to; I need to; I should; I must. Me, me, me. Without your awareness, these thoughts begin to steer you hither and yon, altering your state of mind and negating your human connection. They drown out the song of "we" with the thump of "me."

This leads to anger, ignorance and rudeness. It leads to social martyrdom and public dramatics. It severs the individual from the greater consciousness and leaves them adrift to fend for themselves in a world that is often difficult and unkind.

Bleck. Yuk. Ick. Let's nip that in the bud right now, shall we?

Repeat after me: "I am not the only person on the face of the Earth. I will treat other people with kindness and respect regardless of how they treat me. I will be generous with my time and my manners. I will be a bright example for others."

Sounds like a pretty high bar, I know. But at least a high bar is easier to limbo under. We all have this ability. We were all taught the basic manners of social cooperation. It's not like I'm throwing anything new at you here, people. But maybe it is something that has a little dust on it, and that's okay. It's not a concept that ever fully abandons you, even when you aren't acting within its boundaries. So take a minute to rediscover that which lives within each of us. Please.
Thank you. A smile for a stranger. Respecting your elders. Patience. Connection.

That one is so important I'll say it again. Connection. Because, in all likelihood, that person ticking you off isn't really trying to do it. They're lost in me land and can't find their way out. Remember that and take a breath. Connect with them and understand. You'll feel a thousand times better about it than if you let yourself spin out into annoyance.

We're all in the same boat trying to be happy. How about we try rowing it together?

51

Sometimes the teachings of yoga are so complex that they leave me pondering in circles for weeks. At other times, I find them so simply naïve that the modern cynic in me rises with a sarcastic, "Yea. Right." But, despite my all too human reactions, I find that the teachings are eventually proven true in one obvious way or another.

There is a reason why people have been studying it for over five thousand years.

I recently came across just one such simple idea while studying the wisdom of Yogi Bhajan, the father of Kundalini Yoga in the West. Kundalini yoga is considered the "householder yoga" and is therefore practical down to the very roots of its toes. And sometimes, that base practicality clashes with said aforementioned cynic. I just have a hard time accepting that such large changes in mind can come from such absurdly simple practices. But, again, they can. And do. Such as…. When one is feeling impatient or judgmental, one only needs to call upon tolerance to feel tolerant. Say out loud, "tolerance, tolerance, tolerance." Turn up the corners of your mouth and feel patience and radiance come into you. Simple.

Stupid. Impossible. Right? You can't just change your frame of mind with three words. Tolerance is cultivated and learned, not just summoned like a wayward housecat. Circumstance affects your level of tolerance. Your emotions play their role. Your social training either helps or hinders. So many things converge to allow you to decide upon tolerance, how—and why—should it just be pulled out of the ether with a fake smile?

I don't know. But give it a try. Because, beautifully, it works. And it is desperately, desperately needed.

Sadly, and frighteningly, tolerance is leaking out of our social structure. All too often you hear the phrase "zero tolerance" from our media, our legal system, and our political institutions. And while there are certainly circumstances to which this absolutely applies, we cannot ever forget that behind every action there is a story and a condition. What you might consider intolerable may be a tragic amalgam of circumstance or an instance of differing social ideals. Not everybody was raised in your house. Not everybody learned your set of values. Not everybody believes what you believe. "Zero tolerance" is slamming the door on many people who could need compassion, forgiveness and assistance instead of judgment.

Because, after all, we all live in glass houses. And zero tolerance is a slippery slope towards an Orwellian *1984*. Is that what we really want? Is that who we are?

Yogi Bhajan's theory about tolerance stems from the belief that all human emotions are shared, as is all human wisdom. We all came from God, we all go to God, we are all a part of God. Therefore, the well of God is available to us always. That means that a vast pool of tolerance is just shimmering out there in the superconscious mind and can be turned on as easily as one turns on a faucet. "Tolerance, tolerance, tolerance," and it is flowing free into you. You can use it for the small stuff. You can use it for the really tough stuff. Tolerance is your right—and your honour. From tolerance comes forgiveness, and is anything more divine?

The ability to tolerate and to forgive is the mark of a really great human. It is the path of the avatars, the path of Buddha, the path of Jesus. We all have that capacity; we just need to find it and use it daily to transcend the internal cynic and judge.

It is as easy as three little words and a smile.

I often accuse myself of being naïve. I also work very hard to keep myself there.

Now, I don't mean that brand of naïveté that is simply, blissfully ignorant of things. This is a children's naïveté. And its not bad. But in adults it is irresponsible. I refer to that type of innocence that is a conscious choice of trust over cynicism. I like being there; it is the foundation from which I think, dream and philosophize.

Cynicism has become very fashionable. It probably evolved from a genuine shift in American consciousness from innocence to an awareness of the dangers inherent in modern living. But is has traveled even beyond that, to a place where trust is considered foolish. And heaven forbid you look at life with optimism. That is a social gaffe of epic proportions. Don't you know that the world has turned to crap and the only person you can really trust is yourself?

God. That's a horrible place to be. No thank you very much. Naïve it is and naïve I'll stay.

It is so important to cultivate your trust. One must allow it to guide you. Even in the face of modern dangers, to trust is absolutely vital to health and happiness. To trust is to live within the higher vibration. It is to relieve some of the pressure of simply being a cognizant being. It is to believe that everything is possible and that, surely, things are evolving as they should.

Even when things go horribly wrong, there is something of value in them. They may promote a course change in the status quo. They may simply make us aware of the value of life. All things sad are not necessarily evil. All things good are not necessarily helpful. But to relinquish your trust is to release your most valuable tool of discovery.

It is a reasonable estimation to assume that most people are good. Thoughtless, sure. Shortsighted, fine. But really, truly rotten? Evil at the core? That group is a very small minority considering the population of the world. And treating all of humanity as if they could very well be that infinitesimal group is to deny yourself the bounty of the whole. Go ahead and put yourself into a really small box and then peer out of a tiny hole in the side. This is what it is like to live life without trust.

Why do we think this way? It could be because of the news we consume. All of that bad stuffed into a half hour a day makes for a pretty dismal picture. It certainly doesn't leave room for the true essence of good, which happens in such small increments that alone it appears as nothing. I don't see Dateline taking an hour to report on all of the small kindnesses. "Bobby carried Sue's knapsack all the way home today. Tonight at seven." "Jim stopped to change an elderly woman's tire in the rain. Next week on 20/20." It just doesn't sell ad time, now, does it? And yet we allow this to pervade our way of thinking. There's enough evil to fill the evening news, so the whole world must be falling apart. Yeah, that doesn't wash with me. Don't talk to strangers. Don't pull over to help someone broken down. Don't stop and give directions. That person could be crazy!!

Then again. They could be someone just like you who needs help. All friends were strangers before you met them. One day you could be the one broken down. We all need directions sometimes. You have the gift of judgment and the talent of intuition. You are not a babe in the woods. And there are fewer monsters under the bed than you think.

If you have ever watched a reunion of old fraternity brothers, you come away amazed at the terrible things that they say and do to one another. The words that come out of their mouths are some of the vilest and most foul. They call into question one another's manhood, insult their mothers and denigrate one another's appearance. Usually this is accompanied by some form of physical violence. It is simply amazing. But this is not the truly astounding thing. The truly astounding thing is that nobody is offended. They are, in fact, touched and amused. Hm. Over the course of their time together, during their mutual experience, they have learned to attach a different emotional response to this kind of rude behaviour. We, the uninitiated, would interpret being called a nasty-such-and-such and being choked in a headlock a good reason to call the police. Our emotional response is fear or anger. They understand it as an expression of love and react accordingly.

The same can be said, in a very broad way, of the study of yoga asana and yoga philosophy. For all of its gentle appearance, yoga is one tough, old, so-and-so. Taken out of one's emotional context, it can really be quite rude. Purify your body by giving up your toxic, cultural comforts. Purify your mind by getting up at 5 a.m. to chant every day. Put your foot over your head and stand upright, that's it, now soften and breathe out of your left nostril only. Excuse me? Say what? And that's just the tip of it.

If I walked up to the average civilian on the street and offered those instructions, the instinctive response would be to quickly exit stage left. Get outta there before this strange person follows me and starts shaking a tambourine. But say that to a yogi and the response is more friendly. "Ah, *Durvasana.* I am having some trouble getting my knee hooked over my shoulder. Do you have any suggestions?" There is nothing strange, or absurd about it. The love of yoga is there, so these difficult requests are understood as an opportunity.

Our emotional affiliation to a communication determines how we will respond to it regardless of the words or tones employed. Or, in other words, you only hear what you want to hear.

I don't believe that anybody is wholly immune. Ye olde average Joe is pretty well caught up in his or her own emotional web. All of our intellectual intake is filtered through it—positive, negative or neutral. Like a light switch, certain topics set off this emotional beacon and we subconsciously decide—almost immediately—whether or not we will accept the message. We are all capable of dismissing what we don't emotionally respond to as "utter tripe". Even the most disciplined of scientists, teachers and philosophers.

One can begin to break this habit by cultivating a neutral mind, by finding this emotional 'switch' and becoming aware of what flips it. This begins with an examination of the self, a careful study of the many thoughts that flit across the surface of the mind. You may become surprised at some of the beliefs you hold—remnant teachings from your childhood, fears that lie beneath the surface, or old attachments that you never consciously acknowledge. You must become an archaeologist of self and dig out those autonomic emotional responses, replacing them with neutral awareness. Then and only then can you begin to hear the core message that is being offered to you.

You may still not agree. And that's absolutely fine. But at least then your response will be an intellectually informed one and not just a 'knee-jerk' offense. That kind of blindness does you no favours in the course of your evolution.

We're not here to be right all of the time. Believe me, I know.

I am a big fan of women's wisdom. Wives tales, folk lore, ancient goddess myth, grandma's remedies…You name it. I'll call my mother before I'll call the doctor. I'll ask grandma before I ask the preacher. I'll talk to my best friend before I involve the shrink. My women are the foundation of my wisdom and I am forever rooted in the lineage of their intuition.

I could not be more grateful.

This could be the result of my upbringing, of my personal lineage. The only daughter of a single mom. She, the youngest daughter of a postman's wife. She, the eldest daughter of a peasant immigrant. The women of my family ruled the roost and cared for their children with the barest of means. Half of a potato to cure a wart was by far more practical than a visit to the doctor. Counting the days of the moon was birth control. Vacuums for earaches, showers for colic, these things were passed down from mother to mother to mother, to me.

But not only practical things travel down the line of women. How to intuit, how to trust, how to love. How to be strong but not hard. How to share. How to connect. How to give. How to be happy with what is. How to be feminine and still be a butt-kickin' lady.

I am the woman's woman.

Sometimes it surprises me, then, that I chose yoga as my life's devotion. In it's purest form, it is a very masculine science. It is rooted in masculine thought processes, and has a masculine hierarchical system. There are rules and observances. There is austerity and discipline. You must sacrifice earthly taints and think only of the divine. Guru knows best, so shut up and listen.

Information is not imparted with warmth or kindness. To a Guru, you are the student and know nothing. Your feelings in this do not matter. True yoga does not bring you into a mother's embrace and calmly explain how to find joy, peace and happiness. Always with your very best interests at heart, you are told what needs to be done in order to achieve a specific goal.

That, to me, is not the women's way. Women sense. We think in a circular pattern. We care deeply for the feelings of others and try to bring about positive change with support and encouragement. So, what, then, am I doing?

What an excellent question. And one that I try to answer every day. I take my yoga into my heart and shape it, mould it into what I need it to be. I don't need the hard line. I don't need rigidity. And I don't believe that most of us do, either. Yes, discipline is good. But the roundness of my femininity does not fit into a tightly controlled square box. It is too big, too soft, too full of irreverent good-humour. There are so many things in life to enjoy. And that enjoyment does not prevent me from traveling the path of enlightenment. I believe that one should find joy in the process as well as the goal. I have often felt that yoga needs to have a little more fun with itself. It needs to soften up, intuit more and proscribe less. It needs to allow its feminine to shine.

This is nigh on blasphemy to true yogis. To the millions of hard-line practitioners who wake up at 5 am every morning to chant devotion. Who wear only white and eschew anything—anything—that taints their bodies. No caffeine, no sugar, no meat, no dairy, no white flours, no TV, no modern music, very little sex. These yogis live a life of purity in hopes that their pure efforts will afford them a glimpse of the God within them. That they will finally achieve this union and exist in a state of enlightened peace. A place where the taints and challenges of the world no longer affect them, and their karma is clean.

It is a noble effort. But, ultimately, one that is a step out of time. Life is different than it used to be, faster, busier, harder. When these rules were laid down, things were quite, quite different.

A little story for you:

Over 5000 years ago, the people of the world cried out for relief. They called to their gods with tales of suffering and woe. They asked to be brought closer to the divine so that their distress would be burnt away in the fires of true love and devotion.

At the bottom of the sea, in their home on the ocean floor, the god Shiva and his wife, Shakti heard these cries and responded. Shakti felt their pain with her woman's heart and begged her husband to help the poor mortals. To give them something that would allow them to know the peace of god. Shiva agreed and went into a meditative trance where he discovered and laid out all of the rules of yoga. The postures and observances, the disciplines. He doled out this information as it came to him, trusting that his wife would record it all to share with the mortals of the world.

But it took so long. He talked so much. Shakti soon tired and fell asleep, and the science of yoga poured into the water, unheard.

When Shiva came out of his trance and saw that his wife was dozing, he flew into a rage, yelling that she had abandoned her task and now all of that enlightenment was wasted. All of his knowledge was washed away in the water, gone forever. At that moment, a small fish swam over, brave in the face of this fearsome god's rage. Matsurya had been listening off to the side, memorizing the words, postures and observances of yoga. He assured Shiva that he could teach this to the mortals above water. Matsurya's generous heart began to expand, floating him up to the surface where he was transformed into a man. Thus was born the first disciple of yoga.

Not an auspicious beginning, however, for women and yoga. But who could blame her? Husbands do drone on…

This story, however, is a perfect example of the perceived role of women. We are to listen and to observe. We are to heed the wisdom of our men. We are to be filled up with their knowledge and keep it in our hearts. This was appropriate, culturally, to the time. This was India, thousands of years ago. Men were the householders, breadwinners and keepers. Men were responsible for the spiritual management of the family. Men considered themselves the weight-bearers of life and women were part of the weight. Perhaps this kind of discipline fit in with the male psyche and helped them manage all of the tasks they needed to stay sane, peaceful, prosperous, and holy.

But as any woman knows, this is just patently untrue. Today, yesterday, a hundred years ago…it is women who are the water-bearers of the family. We work. We raise children. We manage the household. We cook and bake and see to the nutrition of our families. We have even been known to fix the toilet or the sink, paint, build and generally repair our abodes. Women are the spiritual barometer of the house, mother,

father, priestess, goddess. We have the pink 'S' on our chests and our capes are made out of dishtowels.
I believe that the very heart of yoga is a woman's heart. For beneath the discipline and the austerity beats the soul of connection. Yoga, voided of rigidity, teaches you to touch yourself in the most spiritual and intimate of ways. It shows you how to let go of things that are not important and find the very essence of truth.

You are a little piece of god come to earth to discover.

The process of yoga is the true gem. It is not the rules, the yamas (do's) or the niyamas (don'ts), it is not the strict dietary observances, or the ritualized worships. Saucha, or cleanliness, is a rule of yoga. But I don't think that whether you showered or not today affects your ability to connect with God. I also don't believe that the cup of coffee you had with breakfast or the cookie you may eat after dinner will prevent you from hearing the beauty of divine song. Whether you rose this morning before the sun to chant "Hare Rama; Hare Krishna" or slept until noon and said the "Our Father" is critically unimportant.

It is not the guidelines of yoga or religion that take you into peace, it is how you integrate the lessons into your lives.

It is the process of yoga that affects my life. I observe the physical asanas of yoga because they make my body feel better. They void the aches and pains of daily living, erasing the stress points in my body that distract me from finding quiet. The postures are like an old friend or a wubby blanket. They are there for me at any time, and never fail to offer comfort or relief. I firmly, firmly believe that this system of movement keeps me healthy and hale. They draw my mind away from the ridiculous clutter of tasks, grocery lists, phone calls, appointments, demands, things that must be done. For the time that I devote to practice is sacred. It is my time to be alone. To feel the peace within the universe and the greater connection that sustains us all.

Yoga postures are harmony in motion. They allow a mental stillness that brings you to your higher self. To the place from whence wisdom comes. To the voices of all the women who have come before you. It is the place where the piece of god within you speaks.

I have learned now, through this practice, to listen carefully to this voice.

It is truth. And personal truth, be it ugly or kind, is the only way to a peaceful existence. My mother used to tell me that it was always best to speak the truth. For when you start lying you have to keep lying, and you have to remember all the nuances of all the lies. It is a vast energy drain, and one that will always, ultimately, trip you up. This is especially true of self-deception, for in the end, the truth always emerges. It is far, far better to connect with this truth, to make peace with it, so that you can carry it with you like a shield throughout your days. For when you know who you are, when you can hear the higher power and trust it completely, there is nothing that anyone can say or do to rock your foundation.

This is part of what yoga has taught me. And I didn't have to give up meat to do it. Disciplines did not show me this peace, but a nurturing patience did. This is the feminine heart of yoga.

I observe the breath of yoga because it is the ebb and flow of connection. Everybody--Inhale. Exhale. Inhale again. Now realize that you have all just inhaled a piece of another's exhalation. You have taken into your lungs a part of another persons breath. How intimate is that? How deep is our connection to one another? Exhale. You have just fed a tree, a plant, the ocean. Inhale. They have just fed you.

You are connected to everything, everybody all of the time. You are not separate. You are not alone. You are a piece of a larger whole and you have the ability to reach this whole at any time. It can support you. It can hold you together. It can heal you. We are a community of the universe, at each others disposal at any time. But you are responsible for plugging yourself in. Only you can open yourself up enough to receive the bounty of this connection. Let it in.

Happiness is not about rising above the nuances of daily life. You are here. It is now. We have come to earth to experience, so why remove yourself from it? The trick is to find the simplest of joys. Connect fully to the breeze, the sun, laughter, and yes, even strife. Dive deeply down into it and be a part of the world. You are here for a reason. And that reason could change every instant of every day. Maybe today I am here to spark one of you. Maybe tomorrow I am here for you to spark me. Break time down into breaths and be a part of the connected whole for every breath that you take.

Life is not about floating above in a meditative trance concerned only with the beyond. It is about bringing that meditation to earth and rolling it around in the mud. Laughing at the sheer ridiculousness of the human experience or weeping with the trembling sadness of its finality. This is the cycle of life, and you can either roll with it or be rolled under it. But to transcend this experience is to miss out on the vital connection of living. This is the feminine essence of yoga.

I call no man master and take no wisdom wholesale. All teachings must be held up to the mirror and shaken vigorously, even my beloved yoga. And when I shook it, hard and with determination, what fell to the earth was these few things:

Yoga is about looking within to find your connection to Higher Truths.
Yoga is about caring for others as you would care for yourself.
Yoga is about letting go of the artifice in life and concerning yourself with what really matters;
Love
Joy
Compassion
Peace
Understanding

So, for the love of god. Relax. Let go of everything that binds you, or tries to force you into a neat little peg. Be it your faith, your family, your culture. Images on the TV, or mores from a society obsessed with façade. You are here and it is now. Further than that all human knowledge is moonshine. Listen instead to the voice of god that speaks to you at all points in time. Respect the wisdom passed down through the ages, but before you swallow it, chime it against your own personal truth. If it resonates, keep it. If it rings false, let it go. No matter who tells you it is right. No matter how many followers there may be.

You are a trailblazer through the world. And only you can lay down your path. I can show you where I laid my feet. I can tell you which branches will swing back and hit you in the face. I can shine the light for you. But I would never presume to say that my way is the only way. All I can do is spread my own truth, open my own feminine heart and say, "This is what I have found. This is what has made me whole." That is all that any of us can do.

And therein lies a critical difference between men and women. Between masculine and feminine. Between what I call yoga and BKS Iyengar calls yoga. For some there is the goal. For some there is the journey.
Me, I prefer the journey. To laugh and cry my way through life, singing and dancing and eating good food. I have no absolute right and no absolute wrong. I have only truth. And love. And joy. And compassion. And peace. And understanding. I am in my skin and aligned with the greater consciousness. Completely connected.

It has made all the difference in how I live. And I wish that I could zip you into my skin so you can feel for yourself the difference this shift in awareness has made in my perception of life. But all I can do is share with you, and tell you just a little something that will hopefully spur your heart to find movement, and your spirit to seek.

Everything is exactly as it should be. You are exactly where you need to be. Everything is perfect exactly as it is. You are perfect. You are beautiful. You are loved and supported. Expand your awareness beyond the confines of your body, greater than you, larger than me, bigger than all of us put together. It is completely safe. Open yourself up and connect, join the greater consciousness. Breathe it in; breathe doubt out. Trust.

Visualize yourself healthy, happy and fulfilled. And understand that peace is yours at any time.

Om, shanthi, Om, peace. Om.

Section Two

Blessed are the Flexible

It would be easy for me to sit here and wax poetic about the nature of yoga. To talk about its many facets, its many unique and wonderful properties, the ways in which it enhances life.

And, I'm certain, at some point during our conversations, I will. But today, as I ponder how best to begin this discussion, only one thought rises to the surface.

Yoga, well: It is what it is.

You can turn the temperature up to a hundred degrees. You can do it fast or do it slow. You can spend an hour practicing the perfect alignment of one posture, or become entranced with flowing movement. You can wrap a hundred names around it and burden it with a thousand trademarks. But, boil all of that down and you still have what you started with.

Yoga—a physical science designed to bring the body and the mind into alignment with spirit.

Whoa, now, don't turn away because I brought out the S word. Spirit is a fact of our lives. It exists within us all, outside of us all, and whether you acknowledge it or deny it, it lives. Some people seek it out. Some people treat it like flaky Aunt Lucy with her hippie-skirts and daisies. But the great thing about spirit is that it doesn't matter which of these people you are because spirit is everyone. Period.

And that makes yoga for everyone.

I can't tell you how often I hear, "I want to do yoga because my doctor says it will be good for me, but I don't like all that weird (chanting, music, crazy) stuff." To which I usually reply, "Then don't go to a class that does that stuff." Not every instructor openly teaches the spiritual aspects of yoga. I am one of them, and this is why.

Spirit exists. Its like the big, blue sky. No matter where you go, or how intently you ignore it, there it is. You can enjoy your day and never once think about the vastness of the sky. But that doesn't mean that it isn't all around you. Spirituality in yoga is much the same.

You can have a greatly successful physical practice. You can very easily ignore the "spiritual aspect" of yoga and still reap the benefits. Greater fitness, flexibility, strength and peace of mind are yours for the taking whether you follow the ideology or not. Chanting has wonderful benefits and I wholly recommend it. The philosophies and teachings of yoga have made my life richer than I can say. My connection to spirit is broadband all the way.

But, if you don't want to pursue that avenue, then don't. For goodness sakes, I'd rather see a student focused on the physical than no student at all. Go to a class that makes you comfortable. Try something within your box if that's what it takes to get you to try it. Don't give another thought to "OM, hare, OM."

Pay no attention to that big, blue sky.

Because the first true breath that you draw is spirit. That first posture found with a silent and still mind is spirit. The blissful calm that settles over you after class is spirit. A healthy and happy body free of aches and pains is spirit. You don't have to kiss the sky in order to be embraced by it. You don't have to be yoga in order to practice yoga.

So, you be who you are. Let yoga be what it is. It might just be the relationship of a lifetime.

We often refer to the practice of yoga as the 'science of yoga' or 'yoga technology'. And it is this. Over the course of millennia, millions of souls have taken the hypotheses of their teacher's teachers and practiced, empirically building proof of yoga's all-around purpose. These proofs are then cemented by their student's students until we can safely say that, yes, the practice of yoga is most definitely a science. And, as a science, it can be managed like an experiential formula. Do this, then that, then this, then that, mix this with that and ye shall arrive at this outcome: peace, understanding and whole body health. As a science, yoga is a prescribed tool handed down through the ages. And, in this manner, the science of yoga is perpetuated through time.

This is all well and good and very, very accurate. Yoga science is specific. Asana is done in a certain way to prevent bodily injury. Pranayama is done in a certain way to prevent mental injury. For these reasons, yoga technology must be handled a bit like chemistry.

You can't just make it up as you go along, fold yourself up willy-nilly and call it 'yoga' just as you can't simply toss a few chemicals in a beaker to see what bubbles up. Doing so can be very dangerous. Something might just go "kaboom!", and when you are dealing with primal energy forces such as the Kundalini Shakti, you just don't want to chance it. This is why we call it yoga science. Because it has to be handled in a certain way. But by no means does this indicate that it has to be done only one way.

For as much as yoga is a technology it is also an art. Probably more so. Yoga is deeply personal. Yoga is intensely beautiful. Yoga is an individual's expression of the eternal sublime. There is a certain *je ne sais quoi* to a successful yoga practice that is created wholly by the vibration of the practitioner. This certain something can't be taught, it can only be experienced, observed and personally explored. From the choice of music or silence, from the poetry of the breath whispering through the nose, from the precise positioning of an individual's fingers or toes, the pride in the chest, the look in the eyes, the curve of the mouth, everything—simply everything--is a unique design of our cosmic individuality blurring towards unity. No science can teach this. It is just too oblique for anything other than art to manage it.

Art is the vehicle that drives human consciousness towards the divine. Science may be the nuts and bolts that keep your ride on the ground, but it is the exploration of our art that takes us where we really want to go: farther into the human experience. The art of yoga takes us on a ride to deeper and increasingly profound levels of understanding. The art of living makes us more than just chimpanzees with linguistic aptitude. Give art to your character. Give art to your family, to your job, to your thoughts. Let them be beautiful and creative no matter how mundane they may be. Build on science, but never let it be the end of your search for understanding.

Just like yoga, you are far, far more than science will ever be able to qualify. Just like yoga, you are more than the sum of your parts, or the rules that govern your physical manifestation. You are God's art, living and breathing and walking and talking. You have millions of breaths of opportunity to embody that--Simply by being.

57

They used to call us gymnosophists. Now that's a mouthful. Even if it does a have a certain ring.

This is what the Greeks labeled the first yogis they found. Naked ascetics able to manipulate their bodies into complex and unusual postures—they were gymnasts. No, wait. Not only did they posture their bodies, but they taught philosophies about the God-quest through poetic rhetoric—they were sophists. Gymnosophists. Leave it to those Ancient Greeks to find a word that manages to truly swallow a meaning. I like this. Perhaps I'll start referring to myself as a gymnosophist in polite conversation to see what happens. It can't be any stranger than calling myself a yogi. People will still ask me eternally, "Does that mean you can twist like a pretzel?" Oh. Now just hush. For the record, yes, I can twist like a pretzel. My friends think I am strung together like Gumby. I can do a full splits and put my forehead to the floor. I can even stand upright on my shoulders as easily as I can stand on my feet. Yes, I can do all that. But that is not what makes me a yogi—er, gymnosophist.

It is the ability to do all of these things—or none of these things—in complete internal stillness. I don't know the Greek word for that. But I do know that without that search for internal quietude, the practice of yoga postures is nothing more than basic gymnastics. For, if the mind is still chattering its inanities at you while you are working out that glorious Warrior 2, and your eyes are darting hither thither and yon to see what everybody else is doing, you miss the opportunity to explore the point.

We manipulate the body in yoga practice so that the mind has someplace still to go. We show the mind what it means to be still by keeping the body still. When your feet are over your head, and your breath is easy and slow, the fact that Sally never left you that really important message about the change of plans next Tuesday in Albequerque, and oh, dear, did I remember to call the hotel, and pack that red sweater, bla, bla, bla….seems remarkably inane. Something more important is at hand, say, I don't know…the fact that your feet are over your head? And if you don't pay attention to what you are doing, you just might topple like a timber Oak?

This effort towards internal silence is what begins to makes a yogi a yogi and not just a gymnast. It takes time, which is why it is called a *practice.* After a while, that effort will fade away. The body begins to move of its own accord; It knows where it has to go and what it has to do. The mind follows suit; It has learned to shut up and just be. Now the real yoga begins.

Yoga is finding yourself in a space of blissful silence with a strange and wonderful understanding: Every instant of your life is saturated with God. And not the God that lives in a church or in a book, but the God that lives in your heart. That's as far as you have to go, just into the shining depths of your very own heart. But if you aren't quiet, if you aren't still, if you don't look, that realization will quickly suffocate in the senseless bull of the everyday. It is the search for this connection that creates the Sat Nam—the truth.

Lucky, lucky me, that I get not only to experience it but to teach it and to talk about it. I guess that is what makes me a gymnosophist.

Without the naked part….

The choice of topics for this column is not a wholly personal one. I do not have a list of all the things I want to discuss with ready dates. Nor do I stare at a blank computer screen until something conjures itself up. I talk to my people. All week long I talk to people of my tribe and listen for the topic of the week. My job is to be the mirror and reflect back to you all whatever topic is offered by the collective.

This week I got (and not just from those I know): What does that have to do with yoga? Oh, grasshoppers.....

Everything is about yoga. It is possible to limit my discussion to this asana or that, how to open one's hips or re-align one's spine, but that is not a fully accurate depiction of yoga. It is on topic, but off point. I could also relegate myself to the doctrines of yoga philosophy, Yoga Sutras, proper Sanskrit pronunciation, etc., but there are numerous writers out there that do just that far, far better than I. Again, on topic, off point.

The point here is the perspective. All of the facets of a yoga practice come together to give one a yogic perspective. It is this perspective that has given yoga it's longevity and relevance. It is this perspective that we discuss. Without this perspective, yoga is just pieces and parts. Pieces and parts that probably would have gone the way of jazzercise and Odin long ago. It is this thread of perspective that links yoga to everyday living. That forms a lens for us to filter our perceptions through so that we may arrive at the healthiest decisions. One must endeavour to live yoga rather than just do yoga. Ergo, everything is about yoga.

Yoga is discovering and expressing that which is authentic to ourselves. And then moving beyond into integration. If you are angry, be angry. But then learn where that anger really came from and integrate that understanding into yourself so that the next time you encounter it, the expression can be more than reflex anger. This kind of behaviour leads you into an awareness of self that allows for healthy growth. This is yoga. No mat required.

Living yoga means moving away from the herd mentality and coming to a clear, centered state. The perspective helps you see more clearly that which is true and that which is merely advertising. You can begin to see what it is that you need and differentiate it from what you are being fed. In this way you become the master of your own destiny and can begin to effect change in the world. This is yoga. You don't need Sanskrit to learn it.

Wearing yogic lenses means opening your eyes up to your personal responsibility. There is great beauty and great ugliness in life and we are responsible, each and every one of us for the effects of our most basic choices. From politics to light bulbs, our smallest personal choices have great effects on the state of the world. It is easy to remain ignorant. It is noble to participate in wise choosing. This is yoga. You need never touch your toes to master it.

Everybody does yoga, and yoga is relevant to everything in one way or another. Be it automobiles, cattle farming or women's underpants, yogic perspective has a place in the discussion. It is so critically important that people begin to move into this way of thinking whether they believe in yoga or not. We as a people stand on the brink. Whether that brink is one of evolution or disaster is still a mystery.

In the end, it will all boil down to perspective.

59

There is a philosophical concept in the practice of yoga that has taken me a few years to grasp. I used to resist it with an understated passion until I realized that it wasn't the concept itself that I had difficulty with, but my own personal interpretation of it's meaning. *Seva* or service, is an integral building block of a yogic life. And, as a recovering food service employee, you can well imagine how I reacted to integrating that one. And, if you can't, let me demonstrate. "Service?! As if I don't spend my entire day fetching things for people, cleaning up after them or asking what I can do for them! How much more service can one person possibly do? You have got to be kidding!"

Yes, yes, I know, shocking! But we all have dirty yoga laundry hiding under the theoretical bed. Look deep, surely you can see some of yourself in there. In a busy life it seems that we are always rushing around, doing something for others with barely enough energy left for ourselves. And now here I go with the concept of service, asking you to do more.

But here is where my misconception took me down the wrong path. Service is not the idea of doing just one thing for just one person. It does not always mean taking time out of your schedule to volunteer at the shelter, library or schools. Being in service is not always performing a concrete action that you can show to your friends and say, "Look at what a good person I am. I have served the less fortunate."

Truly offering service is living with the understanding that we are all here to serve the greater good. We can help others without ever once reaching for our wallet. We can be in service to humanity without ever taking a minute out of our hectic schedules. Being in service is a state of mind that leaves you open and connected to the flow of human ideas, needs and possibilities.

For example, you are acting out of service when you pick up a piece of glass on the street. That simple action will help whoever was intended to step on that glass; you have done them a service. You are in service when you let some poor sap pull out in front of you in traffic. You are in service when you reach for something on the top shelf for a little old lady. You are in service when you dig a quarter out of your pocket for someone who can't find one in the checkout line. Service has no hard and fast rules, nowhere does it say that you have to be a saint to serve humanity.

Yes, we would all like to see more people dig in to help those who cannot help themselves. But realize that, at some point in time, that unfortunate one has been you. Just because you have a home, a job, a duty does not mean that you are immune to needing help. That could be a shoulder to cry on, it could be a babysitter, it could be a ride to work. It could be kindness from a stranger when your day just stinks. When someone helps you—no matter how small—they are offering you their very goodness. They are sharing with you the very best part of themselves.

Service is a lifelong attitude that allows you to open your heart to our situation. We all need help sometimes. We all need kindness and understanding from one another. From the simplest to the most complex conceptions of this ideal, we are all in need of its healing, connective force. Start simply and start small and see how far your service can lead you.

My mother has always collected junk jewelry. Bangles, spangles, beads and what-not, you can well imagine how delightful dress-up was for me as a child.

But unlike these days, where every necklace has it's place, when I was younger the jewelry box was more often than not a giant repository of whatever. At the end of the day everything was simply tossed in the box willy-nilly--very laissez-faire. Periodically, I would come to her with a fantastic tangle of necklaces wrapped in a series of knots so intricate they must have been crafted by the Fates themselves. As only a child can, I would hand them to her and walk away, infinitely confident that she would sort it out for me.

These days I am the de-tangler. And it isn't beads that I have to sort out, but bodies.

When properly managed and maintained, the body is a gloriously well-organized collection of parts working together in harmony. Sure, aches and pains and tangles are inevitable, but they are not the perpetual norm. It is only through years of carelessness and neglect that the body deteriorates into a big, ol', stinkin' mess of knots. Yes, they can eventually be detangled but it takes time and a whole lot of effort.
In my world, there are a few things that should just be. If you aren't a hundred, you should be able to sit down or lie down on the floor. You should be able to reach your arms overhead with straight elbows. You should be able to fan out both your fingers and your toes. And that's just the most basic of the basics. If you can't do any of the above, my guess is that you deal with some perpetual form of daily body discomfort.

This jumble of bodily knots is probably the primary reason that I see new students to yoga. Unwittingly, they have just made a mess of things and have brought it to me to fix. Well, that's what I do. But it doesn't mean that there isn't an instant of chagrin when the knot is laid at my mat and I wonder, "Dear Lord, how on earth did this happen?"

I know how it happens. And that answer never fails to irk me. Sorry, I know I'm supposed to be Miss Yogi-Non-Judgmental, but really. When the body speaks of pain, how do you not listen? If you are continually uncomfortable in your own skin, how do you just let it go? Do you not know that the situation is deteriorating? Enlighten me, please. Because I know the answers, but I don't get them.

If you want to avoid catastrophe, the connections must be made. No part of the body works without assistance. If you wriggle your fingers, things happen in your hands. If you move your hands, things happen in your forearms. It's just how things work. Consequently, if you have injury or tightness in your back, legs, hips, etc., you will eventually have problems all over. If unattended, the body will just work around the problem and adapt. Badly. One neglect will lead to another until you are like that mess of necklaces. Hopelessly tangled and desperate for someone to unravel you.

Sure, that can be me. But it can also easily be you. And if you stay aware of your body in space, your carriage, your lifestyle, and your injuries—if you stay on the ball—you need never lay a mess at anyone else's feet. You won't ever have one to begin with.

The aches and pains of life are inevitable; Chronic suffering is not. Employ that ounce of prevention before you need the pound of cure and leave that headache waiting in the wings.

61

I was asked almost an identical set of questions twice this week, on two separate occasions, by two different individuals. This is not unusual. I answer a lot of questions about yoga quite frequently. They are generally the same questions, and I have a stock answer that covers all the bases and usually does the trick.

However, these two gentlemen asked me something that I hadn't ever been asked before. And when I started in on my regular answer, I heard only "bla, bla, bla" coming out of my mouth. I also heard my father—the professor—saying quite clearly, "You aren't answering the question, kid."

It was then that I realized: I can't answer this question. I simply do not have an answer that will help. And that, I believe, is as it should be. So what did they ask me?

What is yoga like?

Um. Well. Shuffle. Shrug. I can't tell you that. It's not because I'm being mysterious, grasshopper. Really. I just don't know what it will be like for you. I know what it is like for me. But I don't have adequate words to convey that sense. And I have plenty of words, as you all well know. The yoga experience is so personal, so unique, that for me to try to cram it into a box of words is unfair. To it—and to you.

So let me try to explain it this way: What is an apple like? I can tell you about it's physical characteristics. I can tell you that it is sweet, juicy and crunchy. I can tell you where it comes from and how it is grown. But does that tell you what an apple is like? Does that tell you about the full, personal experience of eating an apple?

For me, the texture and weight of an apple reminds me of picking them from an orchard on the North Shore of Massachusetts. My experience of apples is wrapped up in the memory of great friends, a nip in the air, flame-coloured leaves and the feel of hay under my butt as we ride out to the trees. I love everything about this memory, even the texture of the cold wind through my sweater. I love apples more for this sweet remembrance than simply the sweet taste.

The scent of an apple reminds me of watching my grandmother peel a bushel of them for her famous apple strudel. This memory wraps me up in the sensation of family and of tradition. She taught me—and me alone—the secrets of this great dessert. For me, apples will always be as much about love and lineage as they are about juice. Apples will forever be to me autumns and friends and family and love as well as sweet, juicy, crunchy, cool, red, etc.

But does any of this really tell you what an apple is like? No. Because you have your own memories, your own associations, your own experience of them. Every bite of an apple is a universe of these relationships, individual and unique. Your experience of yoga is much the same. You have to sink your teeth into it to find out what it will be like for you.

An intellectual understanding of something will only take you so far. You can ask all the questions you like, but there will come a time when you simply have to experience it for yourself. I can't promise that yoga will be perfect for you. And knowing what I think probably won't help you make that determination.

So, what *do* I think yoga is like? It's sunshine. Does that help?

It probably comes as no secret or surprise that I find the human body just fascinating. I would have to, wouldn't I, to do the work that I do? But to me it is so very much more than just the pieces and parts of the anatomy. Sure, it is wise to know how your physical body functions, what is attached to what, what travels where and how. This kind of information helps you to manage this visceral creation in a limited, but valuable, way. But if that were all that we were, we could cheerfully transfer care of our bodies into the hands of those who have studied these mechanics and be done with it. Many people do.

However, being the proud owner of a 1974 Female Model of the Human Body, I have to tell you that if you buy into this version of body care, you are missing a really great party. The human body is not just an organic sack. It is an organic vessel that carts your human soul through the manifest creation of life and existence. And, since the human soul is infinitely large, the vessel that carries it must be much roomier than the modern medical understanding of the human body allows.

Think about it. On a really basic, scientific level (and I am a science dumb-dumb, believe me) your body is more space than matter. Sure, it feels pretty solid. All of its pieces and parts are neatly and ingeniously fit together. But if you go down beyond the easily seen and felt, we are all just molecules and atoms. Teeny-tiny bits of matter magnetically connected to one another through vast volumes of space.

Proportionately, this space is far, far greater than the matter it contains. Our infinitely large spirits certainly can't fit in the finite matter of an atom. So where do you think it lives? This space is the home of your energy, your vibration, your essence, your spirit—your soul. Shouldn't you acknowledge the space of your body as much as you do the visible matter?

Maybe we ought to take a moment to reflect on that.

Moment.

This is why the human body fascinates me. And this is why I went into yoga instead of into medical school. (Where I am sure I never would have been accepted—science dummy, remember? Thank God.) Yoga is infinitely flexible in the exploration of the human system. It allows for grand ideas and outside of the lines thinking. It accepts that dis-ease and dis-comfort can be the result of more than just tangible, organic problems. Yoga works with the limited physical in an effort to discover the grand infinite.

I try to demonstrate this to my students in every class, encouraging them to 'find the space'. I wonder sometimes if they get what I am trying to say, or just think that I am the 'kooky' yoga instructor who simply wants them to expand their breath. But if even one person makes the connection, then I am successful.

It is the exploration of this space that leads you to a better understanding of your body's real purpose. The acceptance of this space is the first step to really connecting with the driver of your human experience. Why else are we here on the manifest plane? To make money? To simply watch our matter decompose day by day? Uh, no. We are here to discover the purpose of our souls. We are here to understand our inner space.

Even as the organic vessel breaks down, the space remains. The space—if attended—remains infinitely whole. It even grows. It never dissipates. It can't. That is it's eternal nature.

Correction—*your* eternal nature.

When it comes to human survival, you have probably already heard the rule of three: Three weeks without food, three days without water, three minutes without air. And of these, it is obvious which necessity holds pre-eminence.

The importance of breath in yoga is well-documented. It is one of the many aspects of the discipline that sets yoga apart from other exercises. Unlike other trainings, yoga places the breath very high in its priorities. So much so that to attempt yoga without a strong grasp of proper breath is to misunderstand the process entirely. Yoga is built on this foundation of breath. A true breath — that is, not your average, everyday huffing that we laughingly call "breathing." To truly breathe is to surpass the autonomic function and move into a conscious awareness that utilizes not only the body's full capacity to process oxygen, but the mind's ability to remain fully present.

This takes a little practice, and a lot of awareness. This asks you to question something that you have never, ever had to think about. To truly breathe is to move away from existing and into living. Making this transition requires a deep recognition of where you are. It is imperative that you understand your own breathing process, taking a firm grasp of what your body considers its "resting" breath. Discovering that point is quite simple. All you have to do is listen to your body with a few questions for it in mind.

Arrange your body comfortably, resting on your back, making yourself as long and straight as possible. Think of your spine as a supple snake, extended fully and resting in the sun. Become quiet. Then breathe. And listen. Where does your breath sit? Do you breathe into your chest? Does the breath sit low down in the belly? Is your breath long and slow, or shallow and rapid? And how does this breath make you feel?

As we move unconsciously through life, we never make the connection between the state of breath and the state of mind. To allow your breath to cruise on autopilot is to allow the mind free reign, without any checks or balances. It is to permit ourselves to exist in a constant state of reaction as opposed to a state of action.

A rapid, shallow breath, sitting high in the chest is essentially the body in a state of panic. It is our primal "fight or flight" response that has taken over and insinuated itself into our unconscious habits. Daily stresses have put us all in a perpetual state of autonomic response and this is seen most clearly in our breathing. Our breath then becomes a self-destructive cycle that perpetuates this very stress we seek to dissolve. In other words, stress creates poor breathing habits, and poor breathing habits generate stress. See what happens when you aren't paying attention?

To break this cycle we need to become aware. Aware of every aspect of ourselves and our functions. The very best place to start is by modifying the breath. Armed with knowledge of how you breathe, return to your quiet place and begin to modify your breath.

Lengthen and deepen the inhalation and the exhalation. Move the inhalation low down into the belly, allowing it to swell with air like a balloon. Now, keeping the air in the belly, continue to inhale, drawing the breath up into the ribs. Keeping the air in the ribs, continue to inhale, drawing the breath all the way up into the chest until the whole torso is filled with air. Then slowly exhale from the chest, the ribs, then the belly. Long and slow, inhaling and exhaling. Take your time. Do this for a few minutes and then listen again. How do you feel?

That's what I thought.

There is more to life than increasing its pace.

Don't credit me with that nugget of wisdom. We can all thank Mahatma Gandhi who offered the advice more than fifty years ago. Can you imagine what he would say today?

I guess one could suppose that life has always been busy. Even before cell phones and rampant consumerism. Perhaps it is the very nature of our existence to be mobbed by the tasks of living. Perhaps we are just creatures in a hurry. Maybe that is part of the reason why yoga came to be…over five thousand years ago.

Now there's some food for thought. Right?

One's yoga practice is a haven from all of this. It is a time when you can abandon that apparently natural instinct for speed and enjoy the flip side of the coin. Slowness. Presence. Stillness.

This is not an easy skill to cultivate. Asking many people to slow down is like asking a hummingbird to only flap its wings once a second. It goes against their grain. And that's unfortunate. But what's more unfortunate is handling your yoga in the same manner as you handle your life.

Yoga is time free of your life. It is never a task in your 'busy-ness'. It defeats the purpose to cruise through class as if it were a board meeting. Forward fold, check. Deep kneed squat, check. Relaxation, check. Yoga class, check. Thank you people, this has been very productive. Next! All yoga moments, all yoga postures, all yoga classes, should be treated with delight, attention and discovery. They have something to teach you. They have an experience to show you. Yoga is so much, much more than just the movement if the body. It is so much more than a prescriptive fad to manage stress. Every motion can give you a better understanding of yourself. If you take the time to discover it.

Take something as simple as Neck Rolls. We have all done them, yoga class or no. You do them in the car, at the desk, wherever. The motion is an inherent one to release tension in the neck. But most people just whip that head around in a big circle, crack the neck a few times and move on.

But if you really take the time with a Neck Roll, if you really experience the entire range of motion a centimeter at a time, you can learn a lot about your body and your mind. But you have to do it slowly. So slowly that you feel like you are underwater. Inhale deeply as the head rolls back, exhale completely as the head rolls down. Keep the awareness on the neck and listen to your body. This simple motion can tell you where you tuck your problems, where you store your emotions, how you hang on to your tension. If you listen closely to what the neck says, it can tell you about your spine, shoulders and mind. How?

By giving you an experience of the self. When you really learn about how deeply your body feels, you learn about you. You learn whether you store your upset or whether you release it. You learn about your fears and your resistance. Not just of the body, but of the mind, too. These things cannot be experienced and handled if you do not take the time to look for them. Speeding through teaches you nothing and bypasses everything.

If you can miss all that in a Neck Roll, what are you missing in your life?

65

I had a fifth grade teacher named Mrs. Byers. She was a perfectly sweet, pumpkin shaped lady whom we all believed to be incredibly odd. If you craft in your mind the very image of a movie-style elementary school teacher, you will see my Mrs. Byers. But she was no ordinary lady. What made her so odd to us at the time, I believe, was that she just might have been a yogi.

We used to call her 'the flamingo' behind her back because she always herded us into the lunch line standing on one foot. She would always—always-- tuck her left foot up under her grey wool skirts and fold the palms of her hands together in the very picture of tree posture. I know this now. But just imagine what it must have been like for a passel of ten year olds.

Furthermore, when she was teaching us our writing lessons, she would always insist we perform these strange hand exercises. To "loosen up the joints" she would say. I certainly don't believe they were part of standard public school curriculum circa 1984. The more I think about it, the more I am convinced that my very first yoga teacher was none other than that strange Mrs. Byers. God bless.

Now, I have never seen her particular hand exercises in any yoga journal. But the importance of the hands is widely documented in many yoga theories. This is because the hands are connected to the body in a number of incredible ways. As I briefly mentioned last week, they have huge associations metaphysically. But they also have astonishing associations physically.

There are literally thousands of nerve endings in the hands that are connected to almost every part of the body. Like the feet, it is believed that problems in the muscles, organs, mind and so on can be remedied through various pressure points in the hands. For instance, did you know that you can get rid of a headache by firmly pinching the muscle between the thumb and first finger for only a minute? Or that you can alleviate nausea by pressing the thumb to the first and second fingertips of the right hand while pressing the thumb to the second and third fingertips of the left hand? Trust me, it works. The hands are a medicine chest all their own.

What I also find interesting is the connection between tension in the fingers and tension in the neck. Those of you with chronic neck problems may need to look a little further south for the solution to your suffering. If you lace all of the fingers together and twist the palms in opposite circles, you will find that the fingers loosen—and so does the neck. Strange but true. Or, pinch the webs of the fingers in turn, pulling until the pinching fingers slide off. Then stretch your fingers as far away from each other as you can manage and reach the arms all the way out to the sides a few times. Now try those neck rolls and see how much deeper you can get.

And for those of you curious few who would like to give Mrs. Byers' hand yoga a try…. Form 'hand giraffes' with your fingers. The thumbs, forefingers, ring and pinky fingers become legs. The middle fingers become the long neck and head. Now make these animals walk across the surface of a desk. Reach the head up like you were trying to eat a leaf off of a tree, or wriggle it down like you were sniffing the earth. Play around for a few minutes and then see how incredibly loose your hands and fingers feel.

I told you she was odd. But damned if she wasn't right.

I like to think that I am pretty tough. You know, more *grrrrl* than girl. Maybe it was my upbringing. Maybe it was one too many episodes of *Buffy the Vampire Slayer.*

But I can sit on my tailbone with my legs in the air holding on to the soles of my feet quite comfortably for an impressively long time. I can hold my body in the top position of a push-up, straight as a board with the patience of Buddha for as long as it takes most Marines to 'drop and give me fifty'. I can stand on one leg with the other stretched straight out to the side—shoulder height—without shaking and coach others into this strangely comfortable position. I'm strong as a freakin' ox. That makes me pretty tough.

My husband thinks I am a wuss.

He can stand in front of a set of five hundred degree ovens and a dozen gas burners and co-ordinate seven other sweaty guys into an oddly beautiful choreographed dance that will somehow miraculously provide four hundred people with gourmet meals. Without losing his temper. This apparently makes him a 'tough guy'. But he cannot stand on one foot longer than it takes him to scratch his calf with his toes. (The pansy.)

My mother was a single mother in the eighties when there was still stigma attached to the condition. She never lost her sense of humour, managed to house, feed, and clothe us quite nicely and learned how to fix her own toilet. She is fearless about wielding power tools that make contractors grunt and her husband cringe. Mom's a pretty tough bird. Yet put her in my husband's shoes for ten minutes and she'd pitch a truly frightening screaming Mimi and flee towards the nearest cocktail. (Pantyweight.)

So what is 'tough'? What is 'strong'? Is it our skills? Is it our physical capabilities? Perhaps in part. But as I age I am beginning to believe that being truly strong is a matter of discovering that all boundaries are but lines drawn in the sand—easily erased by the wind and the waves of necessity. Once you can move beyond the frustration of a situation or a task and discover your patience with it, you discover that you are capable of more than you dreamed. This is exercising your nerves. And with nerves of steel your impatient, fear based boundaries will disappear. This is being 'tough'.

You can train your nerves to be both patient and strong. It is very important to do so. And while the example I present to you now may seem like a 'so-what-big-deal' motion, I hope that within a few seconds you will begin to see the correlation between physical based movement and mental patience. This is serene fortitude in practicum. (A small disclaimer: Shoulder and cervical spine impaired—this is not for you. Trust me.)

Sit comfortably, preferably on the floor, but a chair with no arms will do if it must. Find a clock so you can time yourself. Stretch your arms out to the sides and barely bend your elbows. Palms up, curl your fingers like claws. Now. Inhale, sweep the arms overhead and cross the wrists--left in front. Exhale back to starting position. Inhale and bring the arms back overhead, right wrist in front. Exhale to starting position. Now keep going—inhale up, exhale down fast like a steam engine.

For nine minutes. Don't think about it, just keep going. After your mind is screaming, just keep going. After your shoulders are weeping, just keep going. You'll see those boundaries in the sand sooner than you believe. Be patient. Be strong. Keep going. If you can do this, you can do anything.

Who's the tough guy now?

Rarely is one posture as imperfectly performed as Downward Facing Dog. Despite my feelings on perfection, which I think should be abundantly clear by this time, I am always chagrined to see how students tend to toss off this asana because it appears simple.

Down Dog is one of the few asanas that act as an all-around gauge for bodily flexibility, telling the practitioner about the condition of almost every muscle and joint in the entire system. To learn to hear your body in this posture is to discover your own points of tension and resistance. To find your own holding patterns in both body and mind. To practice Down Dog is to learn the importance of breath as it relates to effort within rest. Down Dog is a lynchpin pose, critical to any practice and uniquely valuable all on its own. It is, in short, the perfect posture.

Downward Facing Dog, sometimes called inverted 'V', places both the hands and feet wide away on the floor with the tail raised to the sky. Simple, right? Yet, despite this inherent simplicity, there are so many adjustments to be made in this position that a student can become confused if they do not approach the posture with full awareness and due diligence. You have to know where your body is and what, exactly, it is doing to reap the benefits. Practiced without this effort towards awareness, Down Dog is a tiring struggle.

It is important not to mistake the perfect posture with the perfect attempt at posture. Not everybody can get into an asana exactly right. And, as I have said before, that is not my focus. But to recognize that there is a right and a wrong way to try is critical. This hinges on knowing yourself, your limitations and your expectations, and then finding the mean line between them. Using a posture like Down Dog is an excellent way to discover this.

Let's give it a go, shall we?

Bring your body into a push-up position. Orient the wrists beneath the shoulders and feel the strength of the toes in the earth. The body is long and strong here, not sagging down in the middle. Take a moment to feel this strength in the body and the mind. Breathe slowly and completely. On an exhalation jackknife the hips into the air, bringing yourself into Downward Facing Dog. And then we adjust.

The length of forefinger and thumb is pressed into the floor. The fingers are spread wide with the middle finger pointed forward. The hands will root you into your posture. Now we need to lift, lengthen and push back. So bringing the weight of the body out of the wrists, lengthen the arms from wrist to shoulder, lightening the load that the hands carry. Soften the shoulders, and expand the shoulder blades. You want to feel a sensation of breadth in the chest and back. This soft opening allows the chest to press back towards the thighs. The spine lengthens behind you from neck to tail and then presses up. I like to think of Mickey Mouse's Pluto before he leaps, tail pointing to the air like an eager antenna. Soften tension from the knees and allow the heels to relax towards the earth. You should feel and all-over body stretch and a sense of expansion that travels from the mind to the soles of the feet. Every inch of you is communicating.

So rest. And breathe. And listen. What does your body have to say to you?

The answer is what yoga asana is all about.

Sometimes, when I'm in front of a class, I wonder if the students are looking at me and thinking, "When are we going to get to the *real* postures?"

There is an emerging image of yoga, perpetuated by the recent onslaught of yoga-themed advertising, that presents yoga classes as a bunch of skinny women twisted into impossibly beautiful positions. Even those who have no relationship to yoga at all could probably identify any number of asana simply from this type of media. Warrior. Dancer. Headstand. Tree.

But as I've said before (and surely will again) the stark truth is that yoga is not all twisty asana. It is not all lithe grace and the lovely flexibility of the ultimate pose. Much of the time, yoga is about the transition. It is about the spaces in between these fantastic postures. When it comes to a strong practice, it is not necessarily as much about the destination as it is the process of getting there. And I so want my students to get that when they are waiting for their perfect Warrior to arrive.

Think about it. We are all of us always in a state of transition. Those diamond moments of completion are rare and fleeting. Those perfect instances of achievement only come around once in a while. That's what makes them so incredibly moving. So special. The rest of our days are spent in movement, getting ourselves from one place to another so that we can eventually experience that sense of completion. We live in the transition.

Sometimes, the transition *is* the posture. There is no such posture as "Runner's Lunge" and yet you'll see it in classes. It is one method to get your feet into position for a possibly more 'significant' asana. But that doesn't mean that it has no yogic worth. This position has great value in terms of opening hips, lengthening leg muscles, and creating balance. Furthermore, it has great subtle value. The runner's lunge creates a feeling of motion in stillness. It is the physical representation of being "ready to go". From the runner's lunge you can get practically anywhere.

If one can find the significance in every transitory posture, one can gain a greater understanding of yoga asana as a whole. Many think a good practice is one in which certain postures are visited in a certain order. I like a practice where one can experience the flow between the poses. Where one can sense that, yes, being in the asana feels good. But getting to the asana feels better. Riding that moment is an amazing expression of being free.

That freedom can be found in every moment if you take the time to see it.

Every yoga class is representative of life in microcosm. Sometimes we achieve. Sometimes we don't. But mostly it is about the work, the act of doing. Yoga lets you experience that work as life-giving. It allows you to meditate on motion and stillness and the transition between the two. A yoga class helps you to see the true nature of life; It helps you find the moment. And it teaches you that life is not necessarily about the end-game. Just as yoga is not about the final achievement of the perfect posture. Yes, it is empowering to get there, but the journey often proves to be more enlightening.

Transition is the nuts and bolts of our existence. If we are always looking ahead, waiting for something to happen that is perfect and right, we will miss out on the simple joys of being here. Sometimes, it is the place in between achievements that holds the key. And if we can find equal joy and value in that, then we can truly unlock the secrets of life.

There are many yoga instructors who will tell you that a yoga class is not complete without at least one round of Sun Salutations. I would hazard to disagree with that.

However, I will say, that knowing the Sun Salute is to own the perfect vinyasa flow for any situation. Limited time? Short on space? Don't have a mat? Then work through a few rounds of this flow and you have covered enough of the yoga bases to fell refreshed, relaxed and recharged.

Originally, the Sun Salutation was a method of honouring the sun. Obviously. Practitioners would rise in the morning and offer this greeting to the provider of life, light and food. The motions were not only good for the body, but a devotion for the spirit. I've known teachers who have applied all kinds of prayer to the Sun Salute, including "Our Father", but, at its heart, this Salute is a way to give tribute to that with which we could not exist.

As old as the practice of yoga itself, the Sun Salute varies with the teacher. And, there are so many variations to the flow that to claim there is only one proper way is like saying that only vanilla ice cream really qualifies as ice cream. This is the way that I was taught, and its not always the version that I teach, but out of respect for my teacher it will be the method I share here.

Stand in Mountain Posture with your feet rooted into the floor, weight evenly distributed between all four corners of the foot. Feel the legs lighten, as if you were being lifted by a string connected to the top of your head. This expands the spine and draws the tail into alignment. Bring the hands into prayer position, palms together before the heart. Inhale.

Exhale, turn the fingertips towards the floor and hinge forward from the hips, bringing the hands to the floor. Flatten out the palms and scoop up the earth, inhaling to bring the earth up to the sky, reaching the arms overhead and arching back. Exhale, hinge forward again, laying the hands on the floor on the outside of the feet.

Inhale, step back with the right foot into a long runners lunge, dropping the knee to the floor and releasing the top of the right foot to the earth. This brings your left knee into alignment over your left ankle. Press the right hip forward. Exhaling, bring the left foot back next to the right foot so that the body comes into Plank position. Its like a boy's push-up position with a strong, firm core. Inhale.

Exhale, release the knees and feet to the floor and shift the hips back. Inhaling, drop the chest and chin towards the floor, sliding them forward and through the hands until you can drop your lower belly on the earth and press yourself up into an Upward-facing Dog posture. Here the arms are straight with the wrists situated beneath the shoulders. The chest is lifted and the shoulders are dropped and tucked back. Look gently to the sky. Exhale, lift the hips and jackknife into a Downward-facing Dog, bringing the body into a 'v' shape, pressing back through the legs and spine. Rest here for a few breaths. Inhaling, step forward with the left foot into that same lunge, dropping the knee to the floor. Exhale, bring the right foot forward, straightening the knees and hanging in a Standing Forward Fold. Inhale and roll up the length of the spine, reach the arms out to the sides, sweeping them overhead to arch back. Exhale, bring the hands back to prayer position.

Whew! Think you're done? Not so fast, buddy. That was only half of one round. Do the whole thing to the other side and then you can call it complete. And you thought I was kidding when I said it could be all that you need.

Some of the most powerful yoga postures are the ones that make you feel the most ridiculous. They are the ones that leave you open and vulnerable, questioning your position in space. They make you wonder whether you are making a fool of yourself and if anyone noticed. Am I doing this right? Can anybody see how stupid I look? Did you see that jiggle?

I always thought this was part of Yoga's great sense of humour. As if, in their quest to discover health and light, the yogis of yore stumbled upon the silliest methods to transcendence. Of course, this is only speculation, but when you find yourself bum over teakettle with your nose in places it just shouldn't go, huffing a fire- breath to cleanse the mind, well… I wonder.

And then I realize that the joke is on me. Or, on my ego, more precisely. And that it is no joke at all.

It is only in abandoning that sense of self-consciousness that we can begin to move forward. That we can forget about how we appear and really work on Who We Are. This is a life lesson wrapped up in a Deep-kneed Squat. It is wisdom folded into Knee-to Ear Posture. Yoga takes you beyond your surface self and into the deeper realms of your awareness. This transition of consciousness cannot happen if you continue to remain concerned with aligning yourself to what everybody else is doing. Or, more precisely, what you think everybody else thinks you should be doing. Goodness, what a messy thought. No wonder it needs to get out of the way.

We spend so much time worried about our external lives that the inner wisdom gets shunted to the side. Without this inner knowledge, we have no hope of connecting, or learning what our highest purpose is. And without this connection, we can easily be mislead down paths that are not healthy, peaceful or true. The path of self-delusion is filled with the appearances of 'others', the attitude of 'others', their 'other' perceptions of you. The path of self-delusion does not ask you to question yourself. It relies on your blind willingness to go where you are led.

Questioning yourself and your place in the Universe is not comfortable. It does not make you feel all warm and fuzzy. Truly questioning your purpose is very much like a Deep-Kneed Squat—it puts all your secret business out in the open. Everything you try to squirrel away, everything you want to hide comes right on out to look you in the face. And when it does, you have to find the peace in that. You cannot wonder what the person next to you can see, or think, or smell, or hear, whatever.

That stranger's judgment is not more important than your own experience. It does not matter what they think. It does not matter what anybody thinks. It matters what you learn from your discomfit. What you know about yourself that you did not know before.

And the yogis learned that. They passed it on through centuries of yoga asanas. Our earthly awareness begins with our bodies. It is our first identifier. If we experience a challenge in the body, we can use that experience to challenge the mind. And, ultimately, we can use that to challenge the spirit back into a higher place. It is a process of integration that begins from the bottom up, from the body to the light. This is not an easy process, or necessarily a fun one. But it is critical if we are to lead full, liberated lives.

This can happen only when the ego is out of the way. So, toss your legs over your head. Roll around like a happy baby. Put your nose in places it doesn't belong. Embrace the vulnerability of sublime ridiculousness. Adore the space that exposure has left you.

It's a powerful experience, and one of yoga's many gifts to you.

71

No man is an island. Nothing exists in a vacuum. Naught functions in isolation.

As much as we may feel that, at times, we are all on our own out in the big, bad world, it is simply, patently untrue. We live in a world of interwoven relationships from the most complex and misunderstood to the most basic and elemental.

This is a hard thing to comprehend as we are inherently self-contained creatures. We live within our skins, physically, emotionally and intellectually. These internal systems are what support our existence and create our perception of life. This type of perception can only be understood from our ego perspective which can lead us to behave as if we are the primary actor of our world, reliant on nothing else. Do you follow?

This is a false perception. Were you only connected to yourself, completely self-sustained and functioning in isolation, you would go hungry very quickly, lose your mind in a week and have the intelligence of a toad-stool. You are what you are because of the web of relationships that feed you, love you and teach you. Every facet of your existence is tied to another, and another, and another.

Yoga begins to teach you this on a very basic, and easily understood, level. It starts within that skin of perception, demonstrating the interconnectivity of the body to itself so that you can eventually expand your consciousness outside of the body, connecting to everything else. Try this simple experiment to better understand.

Sit on the floor with your shoes off. (If your back curls behind you, place a folded blanket under your hips until it straightens out.) Bring the soles of your feet together and scoot your heels as close to the pubic bone as you can manage without rounding your back. Interlace your fingers together—making a basket-- and tuck the palms underneath the toes. Sit up straight and tall and relax your shoulders. This is called Cobbler Position as this is how Indian cobblers used to create and repair shoes.

From this position, it is quite obvious that the hips are trying to open and expand. It is easily discernable that the inner thighs are lengthening. But there is so much more happening. If you forge the primary connection—hips--then you can work your way through other connections until you realize that very nearly every piece of the body is involved somehow. Your whole system is participating whether you are aware of it or not.

The pelvis has tilted slightly forward to facilitate the opening of the hips. The movement of the lower belly with breath is helping to expand your thighs. Tension in the knees will affect the position of the toes, which affects the positioning of the hands, which affects the tension of the shoulders, which affects the neck, back and head. This tension can also work backwards, starting from the shoulders down. Like a domino effect it travels through the whole system, affecting not only the physical body, but the emotional body and the mind. You may become frustrated which can then affect the breath, which affects the body, and so on. If you find you are struggling, search the connections; follow the struggle to the root. You might be surprised.

This is a visceral demonstration of our cosmic situation. Interconnectivity is the truth of life. Nothing functions in isolation, not you, not the earth, not the smallest quantum atom. When you choose to accept that, a great respect emerges for all life from the bacteria to the biologist. To care for them all as you would care for yourself *is* to care for yourself.

For who knows what small loss might mean the death of us all?

It's good to have goals. I wouldn't even dream of disputing that. But in our quest to achieve, we often forget about the importance of being where we are, even if it is just for a brief moment of observation. Life happens in instants, in breaths, and if our eye is always on the prize, then we are not looking at the present moment and hearing what it has to teach us. And that simple instant, that precious moment, could hold the key to an understanding that has the power to change our perceptions.

Take, for instance, my favorite yoga posture, the Forward Fold. As an instructor, I have always felt this posture epitomized the goal/moment dichotomy. Of all postures, it is the one that appears to be the simplest. Not so. Many people make the mistake of believing that it is simply an effort to touch the toes. Easy, right? Just park your bum on the floor and reach for those toes. Reach for the goal; get those toes.

Go ahead, give it a try. Sit on the floor with your legs extended in front of you, feet next to one another, knees relaxed in the earth. Sit up straight, shoulders in line over hips, spine long and straight. Now reach for those toes. What happens? If you're like most people, you can't get to the toes. But you'll pull your body this way and that trying to achieve that goal . Your shoulders will crunch up next to your ears, your spine will round and hunch. Maybe your knees came up off of the ground. Do you feel like this did any good? Do your hamstrings feel any longer? Does your body feel relaxed?

Don't lie. I'm a professional. I already know the answer.

This posture is a perfect lesson in letting go of the goal and enjoying the journey. The forward fold is one asana, or pose, that offers an opportunity to exist in the moment and surrender to it, to enjoy the process of getting there. The truth is, it doesn't matter if you ever touch your toes. It only matters how you try.

Now, try it my way. Get back into position and bring the body into alignment. Lengthen the spine. But this time, place the palms on the thighs. As you inhale, lift the spine up out of the pelvic bowl, expanding it all the way to the crown of the head. Now, keeping the head in line with the spine, exhale, pressing the torso forward to hinge from the hip.

Keep the legs straight. You should feel as if the heart is reaching for the knees, leading the body forward and then down. You are folding, not rounding. When you have come to your fullest extension (believe me, you'll know when this happens) extend the arms comfortably and grab on to whatever you can get.

If you reach the knees: fantastic! If you catch the calves: perfection! If you reach the ankles: bravo! If you do manage to catch the toes, I'll let you in on a little secret: The body will eventually extend further than this. So much for goals. But, in my opinion, the greatest secret of the forward fold lies in its opportunities. It is a posture that challenges you to find form within surrender. Folded over your legs, with the back opening with breath, you have a chance to exist within moments. Life can be reduced to inhales, to heartbeats. You have the opportunity to hear what your body says, to learn where it resists — to learn where you resist — and then to exhale it away.

You have a chance to surrender the goal. You have a few moments to be. How often do you get to let go? I mean really *let go*. All too often we forget that life is a marathon, not a race. The finish line is death, so why are you haulin' at Mach 10 to get there?

It's good to have goals. But let's never forget that the process of achieving them has equal, if not greater value. So take the time to be where you are, existing fully in the proverbial scent of roses.

73

All right, I'll admit it. I have been wandering in the philosophical woods lately. Do you blame me? Its just so darned interesting back there. But for those of you who feel that my soapbox is too tall, my megaphone too loud, and my aspirations too lofty, I'll pull it back a little. Today.

I believe yoga is a practical science. It starts with the body because that is what we understand. Think of the postures as your boat across the river of consciousness. Now, when we row across something as deep and unknown as this great river of awareness, it behooves us to take the strongest, sturdiest boat we can find. Who wants to cross the Nile in a rickety dinghy? Not me. Practicing yoga helps to make your body healthy so that you are able to explore this other understanding with ease and comfort.

This physical practice of yoga is comprised of many postures, all of which fulfill a function. When you boil these functions down, you come to one basic element. The spine. Whether we are opening hips, stretching legs or strengthening the arms, the spine is a vital component in correct posture. The spine is a vital component to good health. So, in yoga, you will often hear your instructor talk about your spine immediately after they introduce the breath. It's that important.

A healthy spine takes more than just standing up straight. The spine moves. It moves in all directions and rotates to an astonishing degree. This is how we achieve a strong spine: by taking it through all of its paces, bending, back-bending, twisting, rotating. These motions help to support the body and also to clean out the discs between the vertebra so that fresh blood can flow into them. Blood flow is a good thing. One of the best postures for achieving this is the spinal twist. Trying to explain it is harder than doing it, and watching someone do it is confusing as all get-up, so listen close.

Sit on the floor with your legs extended out in front of you. Cross the right foot to the outside of the left knee so that your knee is standing and the sole of the foot is rooted in the earth. Cross the left elbow to the outside of the right knee and take the right hand behind your spine, palm to the floor, pressing down. You should already feel a twist. Don't let your bum lift from the floor. Feel connected.

The only details you have to worry about now are keeping the spine long and breathing slowly. Keep your awareness on the spine and feel it wringing out, like a soaking wet dishrag. This is a very personal posture, and your twist will look different than your instructor's.

So listen to your internal boundaries, take up the challenge and explore. Gently. Continue to spiral yourself around into your deepest posture. Yours. Nobody else's. Postures like the twist can be dispiriting. Theoretically, it should be easy. But years of spinal abuse can make this posture difficult. You may feel frustrated or discouraged. Its OK, just try. Do the best you can.

And, no, it is not fair that the lady next to you can twist like a Gumby doll and you can't, but what in life is really fair? You deal with what you've got and take it from there. That's yoga, y'all. So, if you have any questions, feel free to call me. My number is printed below. I always do the best I can to help. Sometimes I won't have the answers, and it may turn out that I am not the person you need. That's fine.

But the great thing about being where I am is that you can be darned sure that I know someone.

Sometimes teaching yoga is like being a chef. Every day you go into that giant refrigerator and look around at all of your ingredients, making choices. Some teachers stick to the menu: I will always teach this and this and this. Like a familiar family restaurant, the student always knows what to expect. Other teachers, like myself, tend to look at those ingredients and pull together 'specials'. When you come to one of my classes, you simply come in for the ride. Who knows what's on the menu today?

However, like seasonal ingredients, a teacher often uses what is fresh for them at the time. It may be an issue that makes a star appearance in every class for a week, then fades off of the menu for a month. I can't even begin to describe why this is. But such is the way.

This last week or so, I have found myself reaching for a particular breath that I haven't sought for many, many moons. This week, this breath has made me so happy that I feel compelled to share it with every student, every class, and now, every reader. This is, apparently, my *special de la semaine.*

We have already discussed the importance of the breath in yoga. Not just any breath, but that long, full breath often called the 'three-part-breath' or the 'yoga breath'. This is the breath that travels down into the root of the belly, expands into the ribcage and then up into the chest. It takes rather a long time for the breath to fully move through, ideally, up to fifteen seconds for inhale and exhale. This slowing of the breath, in conjunction with the depth of the breath, is what produces that calmness of mind that is characteristic of a good yoga practice. And it is this focus that allows one to move through challenging postures with confidence and grace.

However, there are times when a pose becomes so challenging, or when the heart rate has accelerated too much, that this slow breath simply vanishes. Poof! Suddenly, you are huffing and puffing as if you were in a race instead of Warrior. Oftentimes, you don't even realize it is gone until matters quickly deteriorate and your mind wanders into, "Get me outta here!"

Here is where you must meet my good friend *Ujjayi* (oo-jiye). This is a modification of the three part breath specifically designated for focus. When things head south, turn to ujjayi. When you are trembling, find ujjayi. When your heart is pounding and you breath is racing, it is time for ujjayi. This is also called the 'Victorious Breath', quite simply because it will help you to regain control and achieve.

If you allow the tip of the tongue to rest behind the front teeth and then tighten up the back of the tongue, you can start to feel the back of the throat constrict. This narrows the passage of air and forces your breath back into the slow, deep pattern required for yogic control. You will still get as much air as you did before, but because of this constriction it just takes noticeably longer.

The ujjayi breath is also quite loud. It resonates in your ears. I often teach it as the "Darth Vader" breath, and this is an accurate comparison. Everybody in the room should hear it. And if it helps you through a difficult series, put on that black helmet and breathe as if the Universe were yours to command. With ujjayi, the force is on your side. Remember, a fast breath is a panic breath. The slow breath is the breath of power.

Life is yours for the taking if you just remember how to breathe.

Just for the sake of a little philosophical exercise, let's wonder for a minute.

What if we don't really have our own individual source of experience or emotion? Perhaps we are not as self-contained as we like to believe. What if we are simply networked to a larger whole? Perhaps, like a network server, there is only one source of human experience and we all tap into it when we feel love, strength, anger, desire, et al.

Hmmm. That might explain how we can all define something as ethereal as personal strength. Not everybody is strong; But everybody can tell you what strength is. Could that be because we all share one heart and draw upon Its understanding? Maybe I'm wrong, but I think that's an interesting theory nonetheless.

So let us conduct an experiment. Right now. Come on up to your feet (lose the shoes). Step your feet wide, as far away from one another as they can go without feeling like your thighs are going to split open. Ground the outer edges of your feet to the floor. Now rotate your right toes 90 degrees so that they point away from the arch of your left foot. Stretch your arms out from your shoulders with the palms facing down. The arms want to feel strong, but not tense. Your shoulders should be relaxed. Now look out over your right fingertips and begin to bend the right knee into a right angle. If you look down at your knee, you should still be able to see your big toe. This will let you know you haven't bent the knee too far. And if you can see all of your foot, you haven't bent your knee far enough. Keep the outer edge of your left foot on the floor. Gaze out over your fingers into the beyond.

This is called Warrior (Two. There are others…). While you are here, take a moment to experience the posture. Your arms are long and focused, like a spear. The legs are strong and grounded, but dynamic. Your torso is poised between them, perfectly balanced between the two. For all intents and purposes, you are focused, grounded, active and balanced. You are a warrior of life.

Now breathe. Deep, slow breaths that allow you to connect more fully to the sensations of the warrior. Feel that warrior heart beating within you. Take the time here to know what it means to be ready for anything that comes at you. To have a sharp sense of the calm center that precedes the chaos of battle. You are the both the warrior and the spear, the actor and the action. Think about that. Feel it whispering in your chest and radiating out through your body. Know what it means to be a warrior and understand that experience. Focus, now. Can you feel it?

Now where on earth did that awareness come from? Who here has ever picked up a spear or a sword and gone running into battle? Surely not me. Have you? Could it be that all of the warriors who have come before have all drawn upon a common well of strength? Does that well live in a place that we can all reach?

I don't know. But I do know that the practice of yoga has shown me that there exists some kind of great connection. There is some source that enables us, supports and heals us as we move through this battle of life. And, the more I practice, the more I realize that for all of our differences, at the core we are all very, very much the same. Perhaps it is because we are all sharing one heart that merely wears a million faces.

Hmmm. I wonder.

One of yoga's most endearing qualities is its absolute flexibility.

I'm not talking about the inherent physical flexibility that yoga brings to the body, or the intellectual flexibility that yoga brings to the mind, but the flexibility of the practice itself. Its ability to be or not to be whatever the practitioner needs.

Hear me carefully, reader—needs, not wants. A subtle difference, but a crucial one.

Me, I need yoga to be allegorical at times. I love the rich tapestry of myth and story that underlies the scientific philosophy that is modern yoga. I have said before, and I will say again, that yoga itself is not a religion. Alone, it is not. But it sprang from the religious tradition of Hinduism, an ancient faith ripe with story, folktale and myth. And while yoga today does not promote the Hindu faith, these stories are still available to those who wish to support their practice with them.

One advanced posture that I have mentioned before is a perfect example of this. Hanumanasana is a forward split. It takes open hips and a flexible spine to achieve the pose, and, alone, it is a method to lengthen hamstrings and hip flexors. But to practice Hanumanasana without its allegorical understanding is really just an exercise in "See how flexible I am?" (Or, in some cases, "See how flexible I am not?")

The posture takes its name from Hanuman, the Monkey King and loyal servant of Rama. Hanuman loved and held faith with his God over all others, trusting Rama implicitly. When he was asked to bring a ring to Rama's consort, Sita, he, of course, agreed. However, Sita was imprisoned on an island way out in the sea. Hanuman, trusting that he was supported by Rama, lept over the ocean — an impossible jump — to satisfy the task. It was his faith that carried him through.

So, you see, to practice Hanumanasana is to take a leap of faith. It is to allow your trust in God — any god, all gods — to become part of your practice and part of your life. And, no matter what your personal faith, to allow this kind of wholesale trust is to be prepared for whatever may come at you. It is also to understand that no matter how deep the chasm below you, or how wide the gulf before you, you are supported. It is possible to make astounding leaps based on faith alone and no matter whether you succeed or fail at your task, you are successful for undertaking the effort. You have already succeeded by trusting enough to try.

For me, this kind of marriage between posture and allegory is what makes my yoga a foundation for my life. I can remember to be like Hanuman when I feel frightened of a big challenge. I can invoke Hanuman when I approach Hanumanasana to believe that my body is capable of making this long-legged leap.

Does this mean I am practicing Hinduism? No. That religion, while lovely and rich, is not mine. I am practicing yoga. And in yoga, there is room for whatever faith supports you.

It is up to you to allow this into your practice. No one can take you there, and you would probably be pretty ticked if they tried. It is such a personal practice and faith is a matter between your heart and God. Your yoga is only as deep as you let it be. And if you never want to feel this faith, so be it.

But that doesn't mean its not there.

One of the many things that I love about yoga is that it can be prescriptive. By no means is it only that, but within it's nature is a kernel of, "What's the problem? Let me see what I've got for that." And while I recommend a complete yoga program for anybody and everybody, there are times when you can simply pull out something that you need, be it a posture, a stretch or a breath and apply it to the problem at hand.

During the course of my study, I have found that the different methods of breathing are far and away the most useful tools in the arsenal of yoga knowledge. You can breathe a certain way to calm yourself down. You can breathe another way to energize yourself. You can breathe for focus. There are breaths that bring your mind back into play when it gets sleepy, and breaths that convince it to shut up when it is racing. The study of breath is a fascinating one as it is multi-faceted. I have found that there is a breath tool for almost any need.

The breath we will discuss here is called the Sitali breath. I have pulled it out of the canon because it has one, very handy specific function and many, equally handy peripheral ones. But its primary use is for cooling the body and, I figured, as we all live in Florida it might be a nice thing for y'all to know. Aren't I sweet?

I hope it goes without saying by now that when I discuss a breath it usually refers to a long, complete breath. There are some short, quick breaths, but unless otherwise stated, you should assume that a "breath" means one that uses the full mechanism. In other words, breathing through the belly, the ribs and the chest. The Sitali breath is one such.

So we will begin with this complete, slow breath. Sitting comfortably, really take the time to set this flow through the whole mechanism. In through the nose, out through the nose. Become comfortable with the cadence of this breath so that when you begin to move on to other things, the fullness of this breath will not leave you.

To move into the Sitali breath, stick out your tongue and curl it like you used to when you were a little kid. Almost like you were making a straw out of your tongue. Now, some people just can't curl the tongue in this manner. (Somebody told me it was genetic thing, but that could be poo-huckey for all I know about it.) If you are one of these people, don't fret. You can simply stick out the tongue like a dog. Not like you're sticking your tongue out at a mean person, but relaxed, like a lazy pup on a summer day.

Still working with the long, slow breath, inhale over the tongue. Then pull it back into the mouth, exhaling through the nose. Then the tongue comes back out, inhale. Slips back in, exhale. And so on, and so forth. Because the tongue is naturally wet, this style of breathing cools the breath before it gets into the body, much in the same way a dog is cooled by panting. You should begin to notice this sensation after only a few inhales.

This is particularly useful after a workout, especially if you have been outside walking, biking or running. It is also remarkably successful at managing the effects of hot flashes. Furthermore, the Sitali breath is calming to both the body and the mind. So, not only do you cool off physically, but mentally as well.

Now, I don't know about you, but I find that to be a good something to know. Maybe we'll all save a few kilowatts on the A/C this summer. Or at least keep our heads out of the freezer….

Every instructor has a few favourite postures. Certain poses that they manage to slip into almost every class. We can't help it if we love them. Anyone who has studied with me for any length of time knows that one of my 'frequently recurring' asanas is Tree Posture. So much so that almost all of my regular students no longer need instruction. All I have to say is "shift your awareness to the left foot…" and everyone is suddenly an Oak.

I love this posture because it is so grounding. And so relevant. It connects you to the earth and expands you to the heavens. I adore it because it challenges the balance and strengthens one's belief. Belief that a bridge to God is as common as a tree. To practice Tree is to trust that the earth supports you, the heavens accept you, and that the link between them resides within you.

Tree is very simple. Most days. Start in Mountain Posture with both feet firmly rooted into the ground. Try to achieve that lifting sensation out of the ankles, knees and hips that allows the spine to lengthen and expand out of the crown of the head. Think of standing as straight as possible without rigidity. Feel the four corners of the foot reaching into the ground like roots.

Shift the awareness to the left foot, softening the right foot from the floor. Bring the weight of the body completely onto the left foot and the sole of the right foot onto the inside of the left calf. The right knee is softly bent and rotating out. Bring the palms together, thumbs pressing into the heart. You may stay here if you like.

But to move on, grasp the right ankle in the right hand and bring that foot up so that the sole of the foot is pressing into the left groin. This helps to stabilize the left leg. Bring the hands back into prayer position. Try to lift out of the left hip and keep that right knee rotating out. Balance. Breathe. You may stay here if you like.

But to move on…lift the elbows up towards the sky and drop the joined palms behind the neck fingers pointing down. Then expand the hands up and out like branches, spreading the fingers as wide as you possibly can. Drop the shoulders and lift the heart. Breathe here, reaching to the heavens and rooting into the earth.

While you are here think about trees. Connect with them. Could you stand like this for a hundred years? Would it hurt if someone cut you down? Would you want to hold up the sky and hold down the earth for the entirety of your life? And, relevantly, if the wind tore off your feet would you want someone to mourn your passing?

Trees are ancient and precious creatures, revered throughout myth and story as bridges between man and god, heaven and earth. They are the filter of the planet and part of its majestic beauty. Our lovely little town would not be half as lovely without our fine, old Banyans, Oaks and Palms. While they may seem a nuisance now, casualties of Hurricane Wilma, littered along yards, roads, and rooftops lets not forget their intrinsic value and presence. They are—or were—living things. They contribute. And I'm sorry if one landed on your roof, that stinks, but I'm fairly certain it wasn't a malicious, kamikaze mission on their part. Right?

So as you look upon our fallen comrades and pick up the pieces of their shattered bones, stand on one foot and make a promise. Say, "Thank you Big Brother, for all of your work. I'm so sorry for your loss. Rest assured I shall put another in your place."

Its only right.

Ever since I moved out of my parent's house, my living spaces have been small--college dorms, crappy apartments, divided Victorians, old beach cottages, you name it. If it can be labeled 'charming' by a half-desperate landlord, I've probably rented it.

Having lived small for most of my adult life, it has become imperative that I learn how to purge. If an item hasn't been used or seen in over a month or two, sayonara. Get rid of it. Pass it on. Sell it. Donate it. Whatever. Just get it out of the house. Sure, this has backfired a few times. (Read: crazy woman searching madly for those long gone pants--I didn't get rid of them, did I?) But for the most part, this is a habit that I am grateful to have acquired.

How funny that this very old non-yoga compulsion is actually an early manifestation of my current yogic practice. I don't mean that I clean out my closets while standing on one leg, or sort through mismatched dishes while balanced on my head. But I do constantly seek to clear out the old—that which no longer serves—to make space for the new. This is very, very yoga. This is an external representation of the internal concept of prana-apana-agni at work.

Hut-What? Whoseit-whatsit-hummina? Prana, Apana, Agni. Lifeforce, Waste, and Fire.

This is a relationship of balance in the body that deals with one's internal cleansing process. Prana enters the body through inhalation, bringing a cleansing energy that keeps us fresh and alive. It passes through the agni, or the digestive flame that resides around the core or the body. This flame then reaches down and burns off apana, or the body's rubbish in the lower regions. As you exhale, the process is reversed. The apana is moved up and out of the body, making room for the prana to flow freely and liberally throughout your system. It is the ultimate cleanse.

And you do it every moment of every day. But only half-heartedly.
To really reap the benefits of this natural process, one must breathe with focus. Inhale completely, drawing the prana deep into the body, pushing that flame down. Without prana, we are stale. Without agni, we are stagnant. Let these deep, focused inhales be a conscious effort to clear

out space in the body. Really work out that exhale, pumping the belly back at the bottom of the breath to completely void out your rubbish. With too much apana, we are literally drowning in our own clutter. Waste is a natural product of living, but you certainly don't want to keep it around. Exhaling lightly after inhaling deeply is like filling the corridors of your home with old newspapers—good for nothing but taking up space that could be better used. If we focus on our deep exhales, the deep inhales will take care of themselves. Prana wants to move in and stay in, and we want that, too. But if we never move the apana out there is never enough room.

If this relationship between prana and apana is out of balance, we are tired, cranky and out of sorts. But once you get them working together as they should, you can find the body's natural rhythm which allows for peace, contentment and comfort. People who seem 'centered' are managing their prana, allowing it to circulate within the body so that it may constantly rejuvenate and refresh. Those who seem scattered often have a buildup of clutter that prevents this process. Which are you?

Your body is a very small living space for a very large creature. And it is so easy to keep it feeling spacious and comfortable but just cleaning it out. Inhale and exhale, darlin'. Inhale and exhale….

If you asked someone with only a passing knowledge of yoga to choose a posture that defined the physical practice of yoga, I believe they would probably choose the headstand. It is a 'hallmark' posture that is easily recognizable, portrayed in many commercials and TV moments. I forever hear the question, "You're not going to make me stand on my head, are you?"

Well, no. I rarely teach the headstand for personal reasons. It wracks my nerves to manage a room full of people trying to find the tricky balance for lift off in a potentially dangerous situation. That's my failing as a teacher and I freely admit it. I do, however, teach the Shoulderstand in every single class.

What's the difference? Well, Shoulderstand is a balanced inversion with the shoulders and elbows as a platform. It has a wider base than headstand and can be managed by just about anybody. Shoulderstand is an easier way for people to become used to the idea of inversions and can demonstrate the benefits of going upside down with less fear. It is also a posture that fewer people 'give up' on.

I will not tell you how to get into the posture in this discussion. You need, need, need, someone present to help you navigate the waters of inversions. Additionally, there are many contra-indications to upside down postures. You are raising the feet above the heart and sending lots of blood to it. If you have heart conditions, or conditions of the uterus or eyes, reversing yourself will be harmful, not helpful. It behooves you to find a teacher that can help you find the path to this extremely beneficial pose.

So, now you are all wondering why it is so wonderful to invert if it is too dangerous to try on your own.

Think about it this way. For two-thirds of your life, your feet are below the heart. With the exception of when you sleep or lay down, the flow of blood is always traveling in the same direction. Down. And, don't be fooled, it is work for the body to bring it back up. The veins of the lower body get tired just like anything else. If you don't shake it up a bit, you can wear them out. And then you end up with varicose veins, spider veins and other vascular yuckys. Reversing the flow gives the vessels a break. It relieves the pressure.

In addition to the lower extremities, inversions also benefit the upper glands, brain and face. If all that blood from the legs comes down into the heart, and continues to abide by the dictates of gravity, where do you think it goes? Refreshed by the deep breath, it goes into the thyroid & pituitary glands which manage many important bodily functions. It goes to the eyes, the brain, the skin. It generally freshens up the areas above the heart, which also experience the strain of constantly challenging gravity.

In short, inversions like the Headstand or Shoulderstand give the body a much needed change. We have very little choice in how we move about the world. We do it on our feet and that's that. But it is good to change our perspective now and again. For if you keep doing things in the same manner without ever once thinking about why, you are certain to lock yourself into a set of circumstances and lose the opportunity for growth or change.

Completely reversing the very foundation of the body can provide shocking insights. It can be frightening at first. And then it can be vastly liberating. Inversions can show you that anything is possible if you look at it from the right angle.

And that angle might just be completely upside down.

I believe myself to be in a unique position in that my voice is heard. I have the right, as do we all, to speak about what matters to me. Unlike everybody else, however, I have been given a forum that allows me to share these opinions with as many people as I can. That gift, this arena, allows me to share my hopes that everyone can find their voice. And that, together, we can speak loudly and freely about that which matters to us.

I fear we are moving into a dangerous time where challenging opinions are frowned upon. Its not that we aren't allowed to voice them, but I see a fair amount of social shushing going on. I don't know when or how it happened, but it seems—to me, at least—as if we have become so tired of shouting for what we believe in, so tired of seeing our needs fall on deaf ears that we all just accepted that no one was listening and moved on. Somehow our fervor has fizzled into a quietly resigned resentment that we feel comfortable complaining about with friends, but not to our leaders. How did we all just agree to go to our rooms and play with our toys instead of standing up to fight the good fight?

The answer to that lies in knowing—really, deeply knowing—what it is that we want to talk about. There are many things going on that are worthy of discussion. But they lose their impact if they are not clearly defined and aligned with our truest hearts. It is precision and passion that win arguments, not simply the loudest voice. Connecting with your heart's will is the only way to express a truth that will be heard. But, sometimes, we wear so many layers of helplessness, confusion or resistance over our hearts that we can't express our will even when we want to.

An ancient remedy for opening the heart to express highest truth is Fish, or Matsyasana. A reclined backbend, it opens up the spaces of heart and throat, directing the tide of heart energy down into the throat and brain to draw a connection between the three. Fish, most simply, asks us to connect the heart to the voice so that we can most accurately express that which is deep within us.

From the back, bring the limbs tightly to the body—legs together, arms tight to the sides. Press the palms beneath the thighs. On an inhale, with the hips remaining to the earth, press into the elbows and arch the back up from the floor, dipping the head back to touch the crown down. (Not recommended for those with neck problems, do this from a chair) Visualize a string around your heart being tugged to the ceiling. Now. Feel that openness in the heart and throat. Open the eyes and experience your perspective. Breathe in your focus. This feeling is within you always; you must remember that. You must know that if something true is in your heart and mind, it can be clearly expressed. It is your right to speak about it. And if somebody disagrees, good for them to be able to do so! The flip side of speaking truth is hearing it. The ensuing debate will at least keep our connection alive. Only silence kills it.

The words of Dr. Martin Luther King, Jr., "Our lives begin to end the moment we become silent about the things that matter."

What matters to you?

They say that the eyes are the window to the soul. I think this is true. Because, really, no matter how hard we try to conceal it, our basic nature lives in our eyes. You can tell the type of person you are dealing with simply by looking into their eyes. Kind, selfish, generally full of it—all of these things are printed on the surface of the eyes if you know how to look.

But I think there is more to the adage that sadly goes unsaid. The eyes are also the window to the mind. Entire courses are offered that teach police how to read the mind in the eyes. I'm certain even we civilians could pull a few 'eye-language' identifiers out of our hats. With a friend, one can easily transmit entire thoughts with a glance. With a lover, one look into the eyes can be like reading an entire novel. Our eyes are more than just an external view screen, they are an access point to the entire human system that allows us to see more than simply what we see.

Next to the heart, the eyes are one of the most important muscles in the human body. This is because they are so much more than just physical muscles. The heart is a seat for your awareness. It is a transitional point for cosmic energies and an operational center for many of our physical, emotional and spiritual activities. We are all familiar with the term 'heartfelt' and know exactly what that means. But if I said 'eyefelt' to you, I think most everybody would give me a look that read, "Whatchoo talkin' 'bout, Willis?"

So, how about if I used the term 'intuition' instead? The eyes, when used for more than just their simple physical function, are the base of one's intuition. This is because they are closely affiliated with your third-eye seat (between the brows) and your pituitary gland. This is an important regulatory gland that, when properly activated with breath and meditation, promotes calmness, focus and intuition. Here at the third eye we have another operational center for many of our human experiences. Here lives a great opportunity to move beyond "seeing is believing" into "seeing *within* is believing".

But, like anything else, this takes work. As children of the scientific and technologic age, we have been taught (with a sledgehammer) that one should only believe what one can see. The intuition has been dismissed as a non-sense even though, in reality, it is one of our most valuable, intrinsic, biologic gifts. To begin this work—to regain the intuition—one must put aside much of what was hammered into you and trust that the creator has more in store for us than just these five senses and just this one physical world. The world within has a landscape that is far richer than the most beautiful earthly sights. And this world can be accessed through the windows of our physical eyes.

After you close them.

This simple meditation will allow you a glimpse into the internal world. But know that it is just one door opening, and the more often you do it, the deeper you will go. So if this is your very first time with an experience like this, try to move beyond the sense of feeling 'foolish' and trust that the body recognizes what you are trying to do. Eventually, it will let you in.

Close those eyes and breathe very, very slowly and deeply. Focus intently on the space between your brows until you feel it grow warm or heavy. If thoughts intrude just gently set them to the side. Once the body and mind have settled into the understanding that this *will* happen, simply roll the eyes up as if you could look at this third eye point. Stay here and continue to breathe. Something will unfold for you.

And then you will see.

My first experience with meditation came at Yogi Hari's Ashram where I attended my teacher training. Simply put, it was not a pleasant experience. Succinctly put, I hated it. I don't think I have ever come up against such an intense wall of frustration in my entire life, before or since.

That's not to say I wouldn't do it again in a heartbeat.

Yogi Hari sat us all down at his knee and told everyone to think of a symbol—something easy like a cross, something that had value to us. He then gave us all instructions to close our eyes and focus on just that symbol, nothing else, just that one symbol. That was the sum total of his instruction, essentially sit tight, shut up and focus. So the room got quiet and we all sat, presumably meditating on our symbols. (Presumably being the operative, here…desperately might be more apt.) After a few interminable minutes, he recalled our attention and began to ask questions. Of me. Crapola.

"What other things came to your mind while you were concentrating?" Nothing, yogiji. "How long did you hold the symbol in your mind?" Maybe a minute, yogiji. "You are wrong," he said. "You maybe had that symbol in your mind for only a few seconds." I remember thinking, what do you know you mean, old man? You're not in my head and how dare you tell me—the owner of said head—what happens there! And if you can't tell me how to fix it, don't criticize me about it! One, of course, says nothing like this out loud. It simply isn't done.

So with this golden attitude, he instructs us to simply do it again only better. Great. Thanks a bunch Master Yogi. By then I was even more frustrated that I couldn't speak my mind, that I had been embarrassed in front of the class and that I had no more clearer instruction than when I started. And that made the act of meditating nearly impossible to approach, let alone achieve. I was sunk before I even began.

What I know now is that there is no better way; Meditation and asana come through personal patience and perseverance. And frustration is the iceberg that endangers everybody's practice of it. The plain fact of the matter is that your mind is your mind. It functions in a unique and personal manner. I can teach you many things about your body and your mind. I can show you many things about the process of yoga that will lead you to a successful meditative state or a successful asana. But what I cannot do is tell you to do a, b, then c in precisely this manner and *voila* the result is yoga. As nice as it would be to believe, the process of coming to meditation is not like a mathematics problem. It is a bit more like archaeology--brush, brush, dig. If you don't cultivate the patience for this kind of exploration, frustration will loom and you will be sunk.

Come to think of it, kids, this is just life, now isn't it? We aren't given a handbook upon emergence into the world and our guides are just that—guides. Ultimately, we all simply dig our way through life, patiently figuring it out as we unfold towards the sun. Those who constantly search for concise directions will most likely never find their way because there is no one way. Just like learning to meditate, we all have to find our own method for living. Patiently and purposefully. Getting frustrated about a lack of supposed progress or concise direction won't get you anywhere any faster. Getting ticked that nobody is telling you how won't help either.

Seems yogiji knew what he was about after all.

As I was pondering this week's subject, an old childhood memory surfaced. I was, and many of you may be surprised here, a very fat little kid. Other children used to make terrible fun of me, even going as far as to make "BOOM" sounds when I walked by. Awful, right?

My strongest weapon those days was an old, familiar, playground rhyme. "Sticks and stones may break my bones, but words will never hurt me." At the time I felt very proud of my ability to be so 'mature' in the face of ignorant bullying. That rhyme became a deeply held shield that carried me through many a dark day.

Today I know what an enormous pile of poo-huckey that sentiment is. Sticks and stones will break your bones, but words…words can crush you. Words are the most powerful, awful and wonderful weapons we as humans own. Words have the ability to eviscerate or to elevate. Words are how we express the deepest of our emotions, and mean words, ignorant words, or hateful words are more deadly to the human spirit than guns are to the human body.

Conversely, loving words, thoughtful words, and healing words can turn the course of a life. A well placed sentiment, a kind *bon mot,* can bring someone out of the darkest depths. Something as simple as a 'please' or 'thank you' can bring a smile to anybody's face. Something as deep as 'I love you' can turn the tide of despair. What we say has more effect on others than practically anything else we do. What we say to ourselves is even more powerful still. The vibration of these words lasts longer and goes deeper than we can ever imagine.

In yoga, we are given an additional lexicon of loving words called mantra. We are taught powerful words that elevate us to a higher vibration, that allow us to heal on a deep, personal, spiritual level. Saying them, singing them, even repeating them silently, is enough to bring peace to a riotous mind or serenity to a bruised heart. A well placed mantra can even soothe the ornery beast. But ask some people to join you and you may find yourself standing quite alone, as if you had suddenly started spurting satanic verse.

This has always surprised me, given that people will sing merrily along to a song about killing 'hos and abusing women, then strenuously object to Wahe Guru or Ra Ma Da Sa. What?! A mantra is nothing more than words honouring god—and we're not fussy here, folks, any god will do—and holding that divinity within yourself. Mantras realign you to the highest vibrations, literally tuning you in to greater forces. They are not unlike hymns sung in a different language. What makes Wahe Guru different than Amen? Not much. Except maybe that you'll chant it 108 times instead of once.

There are many schools of mantra. Hindu, Buddhist, Yoga, yes, even Christian. None of them will ever ask you to give up any part of your personal faith. Mantras are a supplement to your spiritual practice, like Vitamin C for the soul. Even if you aren't certain of the exact translation, be assured, I promise, that you will never find yourself saying, singing or chanting anything that goes against what you believe. You will never be saying anything that is harmful to yourself or to others. You will never be eschewing one god for another. Mantra is about realigning yourself. It is about using words to their highest and most beneficial purpose and then leaving that vibration out in the world to heal others. Mantra is about faith and love and health for yourself as well as others.

So, in that vein, I leave you with, Om, shanthi, shanthi, shanthi. Om, peace, peace, peace. Blessings to you all.

85

It is often said that the simplest pose in the cannon of yoga asana is also the most difficult to master. For it does not involve any complicated twists, folds, bends or balances. There is no motion that occupies the attention. No physical root to tether the mind. Savasana, or Corpse pose, is the ultimate expression of yoga stillness. It is the ultimate quiet space.

It is so difficult for many because the act of quieting down both body and mind asks that you surrender. That you give up all of your earthly tasks and wait in the ether for absolutely nothing. You have absolutely no goal other than the achievement of utter release. There is, quite literally, nothing at all for you to do. No place for you to be. Nothing to sort out. No one seeking your attention. Nothing but the vast void of simple existence.

Sounds divine, doesn't it?

Traditionally, at the end of a yoga practice, one comes into Savasana. Stretched out comfortably on your back, with the toes rolled naturally out, with the palms curling softly, you are invited to go there. You are given the time to explore this amazing space of nothing. It is always surprising to me how much one ends up finding there.

To fully enjoy Corpse pose, one must abandon the body completely. You just decide that the body is absolutely fine where it is and systematically relax it, piece by piece. You let go of even the slightest tension in the muscles and trust that everything will be fine. And it will be. What, are you going to fall down while you're flat on your back? Fall off the floor? Physically, this is just about the safest place you can be.

Even knowing that, it takes a certain willingness let go. The mind has to decide that it is willing to give up the wheel. This is not the time to sort out your laundry. This is the time to find the place where the frequency of the mundane mind just simply does not tune in. That is when one finds silence. Blessed silence. Blissful freedom from the incessant and often inane chatter that is a constant backdrop of sound in your head.

When you manage this release, you have stripped away two veils--the body & the mind—that cover your true essence. You give yourself the

opportunity to feel the true core of you; to be, if only for a few minutes, absolutely pure. Completely, utterly, absolutely real.
Like a mother hen I've led countless people to the gates and dropped them off. And then I have waited to lead them all back out. You can't imagine the feel of a room where everybody has found that space. Its like a cool lake of peace that I get to paddle in while y'all are out traveling the naught. (Thanks, by the way…)

The Savasana experience is the quintessence of yoga asana. And yet so many students and teachers fail to give it its due. It is seemingly benign. It is tempting to skip it. Who has the time, right? You do and achieve nothing, so some assume that it is a disposable posture. Big mistake. Huge example of Missing The Point Completely.

This is it, folks. Boil all of yoga down and come away with this. Know your true essence. And no other posture manages that quite like Savasana. Because, lets be frank, when its just you and you in a big empty space of you, you're going to do more than just shake hands and schmooze the room. You will get to know yourself like never before.

And the possibilities of that are breathtaking.

There is an ancient chant that often pops up in yoga. It is one of many, I know, but this particular one is a simple delight. Offered at the end of class it is a succinct blessing and a timely reminder to diligence.

Jai! (Victory to the light!)

I find in this simple word all the courage needed to fight for my yoga another day. It is trying to live a yogic life in the face of the modern world. And I do not count myself among the numbers of strictly devout yogis. But the practice does inspire certain paradigms that cannot —and should not — be escaped, no matter how gently one approaches them.

At its heart, yoga asks you to explore simplicity, humility and peace. It asks you to plant these ideas in your psyche and live with them to ripeness. And when those ideals are ready to fall from your tree, yoga asks you to share them with the world. And it is through this sharing that grace is achieved. But not everybody wants to hear, and even fewer want to listen. Grace holds little lure against the power of material delight.

Simplicity asks you to want what you have. Humility demands that you don't flaunt what you do. Peace is the balance between them.

These ideas, however, travel counter to what we live with every day. In our neck of the woods this is especially true. Our town is beautiful and, for the most part, very friendly. But simple it is not. Humble it is not. Fancy houses, fancy cars, fancy meals, Naples is the land of milk and honey indeed. And we'll be happy to show you the honey pot at any time.

I am not saying that this is a bad thing. Prosperity is a spiritual gem as well as an earthly one. But being surrounded by excess when one is experiencing a yoga life makes the battle all that much harder. Many of our most gifted yogis have packed up their bags and left our little corner of paradise for good. Believe me, this is our loss. All of ours, yogi or not.

More people of spirit leave our gates every day simply because they do not feel they alone can make a dent in the mindset of extravagance. And, in all likelihood, they cannot. People who want to orient themselves with their money will always do so. People who want to live a life of deeper meaning will simply have to deal with it. I have accepted this, but some days it makes my heart want to weep with frustration.

This does not mean, however, that yoga has no place in the heart of Naples. For every Hummer on the road, there is a yogi on a bike. For every gourmand, there is a yogi supporting the organic markets. For every speedboat hurtling through the serenity of our waterways, you will find a yogi in a canoe. We are here. You are not alone. The values of yoga live in an army of like-minded individuals practicing the arts of simplicity, humility and peace. We're just not as loud as the competition.

Be heartened, yogi mine. Be assured that a community breathes long and slow beneath the shiny exterior of this place we call home. It is time to band together now, to inspire a revolution of thinking and dancing and light. To make ourselves heard and respected as we raise our joined voices to the sky:

Jai! Jai! Victory to the light!

Yoga is for every body, but not all yoga is for you. With so many different styles to choose from, so many levels to wade through, and so many instructors to wander amongst, it may take some trials to find the class that suits you. This is natural; don't be discouraged. Yes, even I, yogi extraordinaire (kidding), have been to classes that just don't fit. Its not that I'm not good enough, or flexible enough. Its not that I'm not strong enough or focused enough. Its just that, well, that wasn't for me. And what is for me may not be for you.

Finding a yoga class is like shopping for a pair of jeans. You may have to try on some truly humbling pairs before finding the ones that make you feel like Angelina Jolie. Oh, who am I kidding? I'll never look like Angelina Jolie, so lets say: a pair that don't make you feel like Mrs. Moo Moo after a supersized Big Mac meal. And when you find that pair, buy two, and always go back.

My point is this: Its OK to shop around. Its OK not to like a class you are in. But keep looking, and keep trying. And when you find that perfect class, go back. Keep at it. And when that class no longer suits, try another. The question then arises: What to do when you find yourself in a class that doesn't work for you? The answer to that is two-fold. It really depends on how the class doesn't fit.

If you find yourself in a class that is too gentle, or too slow for your needs, I say: stick it out. Even if your mind is galloping away with boredom, press on. For you might be surprised at what you can learn when you are working slowly through some easy postures. The body has time to really experience what it is doing, and the mind has an opportunity to observe this process. Plus, a gentle workout is a great way to refresh yourself without "working out."

You don't have to stretch to capacity, or sweat like a Trojan to experience the full range of yogic benefits. Yoga is about stillness as much as it is about flexibility, or strength. Its heart is wrapped around silence and focus more than it is around difficult asana. If you settle down, and make an agreement with yourself to experience what is being offered in a gentle class, you may be pleasantly surprised with the benefits.

Now, on the other hand, if you find yourself in a class that is out of your league, one that you are struggling to keep up with, you have to ask yourself some serious questions. Challenging yourself with yoga is a healthy thing. Trying new postures is good. But you have to know where your mind/body is, and why you are struggling. If it is simply because you are unfocused, then suck it up, soldier, and drive on. Bring your mind into play and focus—you can do it. If you slept on a pull-out and your back feels like it was stuffed into carry on luggage, then modify the postures, and work to the best of your ability. Eventually, you will come around and fall in line with the class. If you are just feeling lazy, then, tough luck. You came to class, now work it out. These kinds of troubles are ones that can be cleared away by sticking with the class you are in. These are temporary struggles and can be worked through. Just honor yourself, honor your body and work through it. Know what is too much, and know why it is too much. Awareness is your solution.

However. If you are struggling out of sheer physicality, then stop. Stop. Stop. Stop. If you ever feel pain, STOP. If you just had hip, back, knee, foot, shoulder, whatever, surgery and the instructor is leading you on a thousand merry rounds of astanga sun salutations— maybe this isn't the class for you. If your body won't go where you are being told, then really examine your own capabilities. Again, challenge is good. But so is knowing when that challenge is too much. If you straight up, simply can't do it—don't. Its OK. Any instructor worth their salt would rather see you get up and leave than to hurt yourself.

But before you go, really know why you are doing so. Its alright to know that this class is too hard, too advanced and that you will hurt yourself. Its not alright to go simply because you don't feel like doing what is being offered. If you can do it, try to stay. If you can't, get up, press your palms together and bow to the instructor. Then quietly leave.

This small show of respect will be greatly appreciated by the instructor, and they will understand.

I would love to say that everybody who comes to their first yoga class walks away completely enamoured. That, like a switch suddenly being turned on, they fall immediately into a life-long habit from which they never sway or veer. That is, of course, my fantasy. People react very differently and very personally to their first yoga experience. As well it should be. But they all seem to agree unanimously on one thing.
It certainly was more than they bargained for.

That is because, for all of its fantastic simplicity, yoga is hard. Not like climbing a mountain hard. Or writing a novel hard. Yoga is more like being married hard. It doesn't look like it would be, but once you find yourself knee deep in it you realize, "Man, this is work." Even the easy stuff.

For those who are accustomed to moving their bodies in a recreational manner, ie, runners, climbers, cyclists, et al, yoga is more surprising than simply difficult. They have already forged the connection between mind and body. They can make the transition into the yoga process with greater ease than those who come to it straight out of the arm chair. Their challenge comes with the realization that their preferred physical activity probably won't allow them to just slide into the postures as comfortably as they had imagined. In other words, they know how to ask their body to move. But that doesn't mean it replies with the ease heretofore understood. When they reach down for those toes, fully expecting to succeed and come up way short, the first inkling of what they have gotten themselves into begins to show.

Like I said. Yoga is hard. But never impossible.

Those who come to it with no physical experience have a different reaction than those who work their bodies religiously. As, of course, they should. If you have never once given thought to how your body moves, or how the mind controls the body—consciously or not—you plop your tush down on that mat and find yourself on the Moon. You want me to do what? Put my what where? Whachoo talkin' 'bout, Willis? (Yes, I have just dated myself—and badly.)

The illusion that yoga is a 'girly' sport that just anybody can effortlessly slide right into is pretty roughly shattered when you give yourself over to

the mat. The first time you are shown what a true breath is and discover that you had no idea. When you move into a posture you always assumed would be simple and discover that it is not.
I love to see this transform into enjoyment. For, despite its challenge, yoga is fun. It refreshes more than your body. It teaches you more about yourself than whether or not you can touch those toes because it is far more than a simple physical experience. Yoga is hard. But delightfully so. And how you react to it says a lot about the kind of person you are. Ultimately, it doesn't matter how 'well' you think you did in a class. There is no such thing as being 'successful' in a posture. If you can manage to make the connection, and laugh at your inabilities, you will have taken the first step to finding ease in the practice of yoga.

Because it is a practice. And that means it is intensely personal and ever-evolving. I believe with my whole heart that yoga is for everybody. It is the very best gift you can give yourself precisely because it is hard. To walk away from it because it wasn't as easy as you thought is short-sighted and self-defeating.

What is it that they say? Ah, yes. Anything worth having is worth working for.

89

I have always wanted to ride down one of those zip lines. You know the ones, over the rainforest canopy somewhere in Costa Rica. Every time I see it on TV I think, "Man, that looks like so much fun." It also looks pretty easy. Butt in the harness. Hands on the grip. Push off and, wheeeeeeeeee over the tree tops you go.

But I'm no fool. Just because it seems easy doesn't mean it is a wise idea to string a clothesline over the monkey lake at Caribbean Gardens, plop your tookus in a Publix bag suspended over some old handlebars and let 'er rip. There is a reason there are trained, insured professionals setting you up in the safety gear. They know things that you don't.

I have also always wanted to perform the Scorpion asana. For those of you unfamiliar, think headstand with your head lifted from the floor, neck arched back while your body gracefully lifts off into the air. Then your back arches so that your feet can meet the crown of your head. It looks glorious.

But again, I'm no fool. I know lots about yoga and I still don't know enough to manage that pose. I've not been taught and I'm not about to toss myself into an inverted backbend just because I think I should be able to handle it. Maybe I could. But can you really believe that is wise?

Um. No. And I'll tell you why. An unexamined belief in your own abilities is the most dangerous form of pride. And we all know what they say: Pride goeth before a fall.

Pride is the devil on your shoulder telling you who you are and what you should be able to achieve. It also has a very skewed perspective on the truth. Pride is that little voice that says, "I'm going to take yoga. I've always been flexible and I've always been in pretty good shape. Surely an advanced class is appropriate for me." Or better yet. "I used to lift weights when I played football in school. It was only ten years ago; Not that long at all, really. Surely a 200 lb. Bench press is a just fine place to start."

Okay. Reality check. Today is not yesterday. Nor is it tomorrow. A real understanding of the self—and its abilities-- comes from this very moment. What can you do right now? Perhaps it will be something you have always been able to do. But, then again, perhaps you are different and what was once true no longer holds. The only way to know is to put pride on the shelf and really look at the foundation under your feet at this instant.

So, sure, you're in good shape. But do you have the fundamental yogic knowledge of breath and mind control? If the answer is no, then that advanced class is not the right place for you no matter what you think. So, sure, you might have been a muscleman in school. But has that muscle turned to a beer belly and donut neck? If so, then perhaps jumping right back into the deep end of the pool, so to say, ain't such a good idea.

Things change. And unlike a house made of stone, the house of self is always shifting and growing. Your foundations are not set; they alter over time. Do not be so prideful as to think that what you know is what you know and that is the end of that. That's just asking to get hurt—in any number of ways.

Truly wise people realize that they don't really know anything. There is great humour in that. And great freedom as well. This leads to awareness and grace—the real foundation of life.

Now that's something to be proud of.

There are many, many things in the world that will happily introduce you to your limitations. I happen to think yoga is high up on the list of those that will simply stun you with the limitations it reveals.

For when we run across an intellectual limitation, we can easily dismiss our chagrin with the rationalization that we have simply not yet learned what needs to be learned. When we run up against a social limitation, we can simply chalk it up to class structure and the ills of modern society. When we run up against an economic limitation, we can just set our caps at making the money we need to surpass it. But when we run smack dab into the walls of our own physical limitations—those that aren't caused by outright injury or handicap—we often find ourselves simply dumbfounded.

I believe this is because we inherently assume that our bodies will do what is demanded of them. When we were children we wanted to walk, so we learned to walk. We want something on the top shelf, we reach up and take it off of the shelf. Our bodies have always simply responded to our desires with very little thought or effort towards how or why it performs for us. But the practice of yoga takes one out of automatic functioning and into conscious movement. It asks you to perform physical tasks that have no subconscious inherency. They are completely foreign, and you have no idea how foreign they are until you sit down and try to manage them the same way you have always managed your body—without thought to your real situation.

And then forward fold meets tight lower back and your toes are a surprising eternity away. And then spinal twist meets collapsed pelvis and your hips astonishingly rage in protest. And then your ears hear right arm and your left arm raises curiously, leaving you completely, absurdly turned around. Suddenly you have simply no idea how to manage this body of yours that has always performed quite satisfactorily until just right now. Hello, limitations, how not nice to meet you.

Sadly, this is where many people give up, assuming that yoga is ridiculous for even asking you to move this body in this fashion. Nobody likes to discover that they are limited. But I am here to tell you that being limited is a wonderful thing. For it is only when we discover

and embrace our limited nature that we can discover the limitless being that truly resides within us.
Think about it. The nature of the body is the nature of limits. We are limited by the boundary our skin. We are limited by our dependency on oxygen and food. We are limited by gravity. We are limited by our gender. We are limited by the jittery nature of our minds. We are limited by time and by death. We, the human being, are quite simply, limited.

The eternal being, however, is limitless. The eternal consciousness has no experiential conception of time, gravity, gender, mind, food, air, death, etc. It has no conception of what it means to be restricted by all of the things that we simply accept as part and parcel of existence. Perhaps we are here to reflect that understanding back—to help define the nature of duality to that which is simply Oneness.

From this angle, honouring and enjoying our limitations is of critical importance. Then and only then can we begin to work with them to discover that which is beyond them. Perhaps our task here is to be imperfect and flawed and limited. Perhaps it is not only to seek out eternal understanding, but to let it seek out our limited one.

Perhaps your limitations are not the end, but only a beginning….

91

There comes a day when your yoga practice walks off of the mat and follows you home. Like a determined little puppy it shuffles along by your side, barking and sniffing at all manner of things that you had never noticed before. Suddenly, it seems, you are aware.

Damn. How did that happen?

My first teacher used to say that yoga asks things of you, that it is the most demanding of lovers. I never truly knew what she meant until my own yoga followed me home and began to root around in my life. There I was, perfectly discontent, practicing a few asanas to soothe my aching waitress feet when—bam!—yoga peeled off the blinders and, for the first time, I saw. Suffice it to say, things have never been quite the same since.

Once this transition is made, there is, quite simply, no going back. There is no replacing of the blindfold. No ignoring of the truths. And, some days, this is what you will desperately yearn to do. It is far, far easier to live life in a cocoon of materialism and denial than it is to live the life examined. Sometimes the sights are hard and ugly. Other times they are beautiful enough to bring tears to your eyes. But this is the balance of life, and one of the many gifts that yoga gives. It is also one of its harshest demands.

To walk with yoga, be it in full consciousness or burgeoning awareness, is to walk within the connection. In class, we are taught to connect the mind to the body. To be fully aware of what we are doing and why. At the end of class we are invited to relax, and to connect our awareness to the greater consciousness. Simply put, for an hour we are plugged in. We are whole.

Do you believe that this is something that can simply be put away? Rolled up with your mat and stowed in the trunk of your car? Once experienced, would you even want to?

Living in this awareness allows you to find true happiness. The kind that doesn't always scream to be refilled. The kind that doesn't expire beneath the spotlight of adversity. This gift of yoga is a constant companion, a true mate. This demand of yoga forces you to see that this happiness is all around you all of the time. But you must embrace it.

You must carry it in your heart and share it with others. It will never be handed to you, and it is not always fun.

To embark upon the practice of yoga is to seek. It is to begin to hear the right questions and to really think about the right answers. And, as much as we may like to pretend otherwise, yoga is like a Catholic schoolteacher. She may have your best interests at heart, but she's not gonna take any of your bull. Your yoga will shine a bright, brilliant light into the darkest corners of your psyche and illuminate all of your hidden crap. It will ask you to explore, examine, and discard. Truly, you will come out a better person because of it. No matter the reasons for seeking out yoga, you will always find more than you bargained for.

Is this a good thing or a bad? Some days it is hard to tell. Some days it is more than you want. But it is always exactly what you need. Life is big, and messy and scary and delightful. Sometimes, we all need a questioning puppy to lead the way.

My, what visual creatures we have become!

You can learn your history from a TV show. You can send e-mails from your cell phone. You can teach your child how to do math from video. In this day and age, surely, a picture is more valuable than a thousand words—or more.

It wasn't always so. Generations of people were educated by rote. Listening, repeating. Listening, repeating. Vast, epic poems were learned and memorized with metre and cadence of language alone. Whole histories of nations were taught and remembered by ear. Amazing. Most of us today can't remember what we were asked to pick up at the store. The art of listening is lost.

I see this in my yoga classes all of the time. People who just refuse to listen. For years I would get a little agitated at this. *I'm not up here talking to myself, people!* It took me some time to realize that it isn't that they won't listen—it's that they can't. We have bred the skill of auditory comprehension straight out of ourselves. Why bother to hear what needs to be done when you can see it?

Yoga remains a last bastion to this 'from the knee' kind of education. The art of yoga is truly learned only from another person. One who has more skill than you and is willing to let you sit at their knee and hear everything they have to say on the subject. Yoga is learned from the connection of teacher to student. The deeper levels cannot be fully grasped from a book or a video or by watching. And this simply visual attempt at comprehension misses understanding by degrees. The subtleties of yoga need communication to work.

In other words, you need to listen. Don't watch. Listen. You are being told more than you will ever see. Your instructor is imparting deeper levels of understanding with their words rather than their bodies. At times, the eyes can do more damage to your focus than help.
For example. I do not mirror. If I say raise the right hand, I'm raising my right hand. If you are watching me and not listening then your left hand goes up. Well, now we're just confused, aren't we? If I say, "Bring your awareness to your left hip", and you are watching me with your

right hip in the wrong place then your awareness is on me and not where it should be. And now you are missing something.

Listen. Listen to the words that are coming out of my mouth. If I could just stand in front of a class and merrily practice away, fully confident that you understood the deepest subtleties of the asanas and could follow along, believe me, I would. And sometimes, I do. But if I am saying something to you, then hear me. This is why you came. This is how you learn about yoga. This is how you learn about yourself. By listening.

It's a shame that we have to practice this. It was gifted to us with the rest of our senses, as equally as valuable as any of them. Listening may be more subtle than seeing. Maybe more difficult. But listening is a bridge to remembering, a ferryboat to imagining. Try to tell a story rather than read one and you'll see exactly what I mean. Listening is purer than seeing, and if you master the art you can ignore visual clutter and truly tune in. Focus. You may hear and discover things of which you never dreamed.

…..and, no, the irony of this essay does not escape me at all….

93

I hope that by now it won't surprise you to learn that I have a real Sci-fi habit. Books, TV, movies, you name it, I've probably read it, seen it, watched it. What can I say? I'm a geek at heart.

Several years ago I read a novel that was later turned into a movie. Great book; crappy film. (Quel surprise…) But oddly, it wasn't the plot that stuck with me, it was just one great thought. A comment, really, a casual observation.

A team of scientists had just traveled back through time to the Middle Ages. (I know, I know, geek. Remember?) When they got there, one character mentioned how surprised he was by the absolute silence. Those were his words. Absolute Silence. And he went on to clarify that it wasn't merely the absence of man or beast, it was the true quiet of a time when there was no omnipresent electric hum.

Now, for some reason, that thought just set me back on my heels. Because it's so true and we never, ever think about it. There is always something humming along in the background. Not just appliances or air-conditioning, but the simple fact of electric presence in the power lines that spider web our lives. We are always surrounded by sound, even if it is so low as to be barely perceived as such. I guess, as modern man, we are denied the gift of true silence.

As a yoga teacher, I find this idea even more intriguing. We take such pains to create a quiet space, to try and bring the sounds of modern living down to silence. Of course we never succeed absolutely. There will always be garbage men, phones, voices, dogs, car doors, what-have-you. Even if we know that we will never fully succeed, we at least try, seeking this silence as best we can. How interesting to know that there ultimately is no such thing.

The remedy to this outside chitter-chatter is, of course, to turn the attention within. One simply chooses not to hear external stimuli. We still the mind and allow ourselves to become quiet within, trying to ignore that which is not inside of us. But this inward turn can actually make the outside noise seem worse if one is not equanimous towards it.

They say you have a thousand thoughts in the wink of an eye. Think now about the noise that makes in your head. If you've got all these thoughts racing around, shouting at you—for all intents and purposes—then you probably won't be as disturbed by the wail of a distant police siren, or the barking of a neighbor's dog. But once you start to silence these thoughts, as we do in yoga, those other noises have more room to move in. Your quiet self can be more susceptible to the person shouting at their cell phone outside. Their noise can invade your space and annoy you as if they were standing right next to you hollering at the top of their lungs.

In order to keep this from sinking your concentration, one must achieve a rather blasé reaction to it. Oh well, there is some noise. It is as good as silence; I'll be fine. In other words, one cannot attach a "successful" yoga practice to the idea that it should be done in perfect quiet. Because, as we have just said, no such thing exists.

Ultimately, quiet is only a state of mind. And trying to control your external environment absolutely will only serve to make you nuts. So nuts that you have little hope of really finding that true peace and quiet.

The kind that comes from within.

Technically, yoga can be practiced just about anywhere. Imagine, in the millennia that have gone before, millions upon millions of yogis practicing on mountaintops, in forests, deserts, parks, playgrounds, beaches, rooftops, living rooms, gymnasiums, back porches and so on. There is no hard and fast rule that says you have to practice in a solemn, yoga-only environment. I know lots of yogis who just roll out the mat and let it fly. I've been known to be one of them.

However, ask any guru and you will probably be told that you should maintain a dedicated place for yoga. Hm. Hard to do. And if yoga is so portable, why should it matter?

Well. That's a tricky one to explain. Because it does matter. And, it does not. If you have a deep enough grasp of the practice, you should be able to clear your mind to the point where you could practice in a pen of howler monkeys and still be fully present. Conversely, the more open and connected that you are, the more susceptible you become to residual negativities and energies left in your environment.

We have all been to places that just 'felt' good. For no visible reason, you feel instantly at home, relaxed. I know we have also all found ourselves in places that feel wrong. You feel jumpy, tense, or just plain "ready to leave". We humans are very sensitive to our environment. These stray feelings are our subtle awareness of other people's energy.

First, you have to understand that we are all emotional graffiti artists. Every one of us is walking around with a case of spiritual spray paint. Which can we use depends on our mood and emotional state. So, if you're stuck in a room and are pretty ticked off about it, you radiate angry, irritated energy. That room is then going to carry traces of that angry, irritated energy whether you stay there or not. You have tagged it with the colour of your emotions.

Now, if you create a place that only experiences feelings of peace and serenity—say, a dedicated yoga space—that place will remain full of that good feeling. Every time you use it to create those same feelings, you reinforce it. You continually paint it the same colour every time you visit. This is why the gurus say you should have a dedicated space for your yoga and meditation.

You can find that space in a number of ways. The first, and most obvious way, is to set up an area in your house which is meditation-yoga only. Now, I don't know about y'all, but my house is so small that the prospect is laughable. So, my space is outdoors. Things move in the outdoors. It is too big for crap to hang around. By default, it is a clear space.

Another alternative is to practice at a studio. There are a number of them in town, please don't think I say this selfishly. Studios are spaces that are being reinforced with spirit all day, everyday. Can you say that about your gym? Or your clubhouse? Studios are places of focus and dedication. Every student who comes in the door, every instructor that shares their vision is helping to paint the space with the brightest of energy. And that energy stays there as long as the doors are open and people come to experience yoga.

It is, of course, between you and your practice how and where you choose to express your yoga. But it is worth investigation to step away from the convenient and into the deeper end of the pool. If you learn to feel the difference between muddled energy and clear, you will have developed a sense that can be invaluable in the everyday practicality of life.

95

A very close friend of mine recently confessed that she wanted to become a yoga teacher. She was giving serious thought to the Teacher Training Program I attended with Yogi Hari.

I think I might have frightened her with my response.

I believe I likened my teacher training experience to being suddenly swept from your feet, hung upside down by the ankles a mile over the surface of the earth and shaken vigorously until every bit of emotional and intellectual change had fallen out of the pockets of your soul.
It was awful. It was wonderful. It was a pivotal life experience that showed me exactly how much of my life before had been circus play. And it was only once this realization came clear that I was ready to begin a new chapter as a teacher of yoga.

There are multitudes of teacher training programs out there. They are as varied as wildflowers on a Vermont hillside. Some will treat you like a guest, giving you thorough anatomical information needed to lead others through asana. Others will pamper you in luxurious, comfortable surroundings while inundating you with Vedic philosophy. Yet others will treat you as I was, stripping away any illusions of identity with firm tugs until you are emotionally naked enough to absorb the teachings. Ultimately, it is up to you to decide what kind of experience you desire. But you should also consider this: The program you want may not be the one you need.

Deciding to become a yoga teacher is not a blithe decision. Its not like saying, “Oh, I think I’ll wear white today.” For, despite its many perks, being a *yoga shiromani* is hard. You will constantly be aware of what you are saying, doing, demonstrating. You need to continually study. You will always be questioning, questing. You will agree to accept certain changes in your lifestyle and, furthermore, to share these changes with others. It’s a tough way to make a living. Because, while the schedule is great, the pay can really stink and you are forever finding yourself either up on some strange pedestal or down at the bottom of somebody’s nose. Becoming a yoga teacher is something one does only after careful examination.

I encourage anybody who wants to deepen their personal experience of yoga through teaching to really shop around for a program that is complete with asana, philosophy, karma, mantra, meditation & lifestyle. The program should immerse you in the yogic way of living—ideally in an ashram environment. Because to really understand what you are agreeing to do, you need not only learn the asanas, but to have the original experience.

Being a teacher is so very much more than just posture, alignment and sequence. There is a great art to it. You can begin to understand this with a training program that sets you back on your heels, if not your butt. A good program should fill you with the joy and wonder of yoga. But I also think it should rock your very foundations. It should shake loose any rubble of wrong thinking and bad living. If you don't question yourself and your decision to be there at least once, I think your program might be missing something.

Yoga is a self-shaking experience. At some point in time, you will have to empathize with a student who is just discovering that and has questions. How can you know what they need if you've never been shaken yourself? Programs that don't give you this will ultimately be doing you a disservice.

And if you intend to become a teacher of yoga, you owe it to yourself—and to your students—to really understand what that means.

There are two kinds of people in the world. The ones who will tell you that you have spinach in your teeth; And the ones who will let you go on about your business with spinach in your teeth. Which is the better approach? Momentary embarrassment? Or delayed embarrassment?

I always prefer the momentary. Whoops, sorry. Spinach in my teeth. How embarrassing, did I get it? And that is why I am a proud member of the former grouping. I will always tell you about the proverbial spinach if it means you won't be further embarrassed. So, please, bear this in mind as we go on about our business.

I am asked about starting yoga nearly every day. People call and email to ask how they can get the ball rolling. What kind of class should I take? Should I buy my own mat? I try my best to steer them to the place they will be most at ease.

But when it comes to 'What should I wear?', my reply is constant. "Something comfortable, a little stretchy; No buttons, no zippers. Whatever you usually exercise in is fine." However, I find now that this reply is creating a little spinach that maybe you should know about. My fault entirely.

Suitable bottoms for the practice of yoga can be pants or shorts. A suitable top is a fitted t-shirt or a tank top. But. Certain understandings must be applied. You can't just throw on a pair of old running shorts or stretch pants and a giant t-shirt and consider yourself prepared. Going to a yoga class is not the same as climbing onto a treadmill, or bench pressing a couple of bars.

You certainly don't have to run out and buy yourself a new 'yoga wardrobe'. Generally, people pull some type of old athletic attire out of their closet and that is usually fine. But the more of these 'comfortable' clothes I see, the more I realize that some of y'all don't know what your old stuff does when you start moving. Some of those old clothes really share your business, if you take my meaning.

For instance. Gentlemen. If you want to wear running shorts, great. But please (please) wear briefs beneath them. Ladies, same goes. A wide leg short gapes open when you lay down. And rides up when you bend

over. If you are wearing your 'athletic' thong, or no panties at all…well. Need I really detail the image?
I practice in a good-quality, closed leg, stretch short or pant. Because they don't gap and they generally don't ride. But, if the last time you put those bottoms on was 1986, you should be aware: Lycra thins in the seat as it ages. When pulled tight, it appears very sheer. In other words: You can see right through it. And if you have again decided to eschew underpants….

To determine if your clothes are yoga-friendly, try this simple experiment. Put them on. Stand with your back to a full length mirror. Now bend all the way over and look between your thighs at the image. What you see in the mirror is what I see in class. Does your shirt fall so far open that you can see your tummy or girly goods? Do your pants put the 'hoohah' on display? If so, the answer is no. These are not good clothes for yoga.

You want to be comfortable. And that means not only physically, but in a way that aligns with your own sense of modesty. Don't be embarrassed, be aware. So you got a little spinach in your teeth. So you showed a little tushie in class.

I wouldn't tell ya if I didn't love ya.

Ladies, ladies, ladies. I know where your heart is coming from, truly I do. I have a man, too, and I want him to live forever. I want him to exercise, to eat better, to see the doctor without whining like a four-year-old. I wish he would take as good care of himself as I try to, really I do, with all of my heart.

But if wishes were wings, pigs would fly.

So, please take this in the loving and understanding fashion with which it is offered. Please do not drag your husband to yoga class if he really doesn't want to go. I've seen it, I've tried it, I've taught it. It's a freaking nightmare. Now, feel free to cajole and harass him. Needle and nag to your heart's content. I did. It didn't get me very far—but then, my husband is a mule, so I've long since given up.

Yoga will help your man in more ways than he can know. We understand that. It will keep him healthy for many years to come. We want that. But it will only be so if it is something that he wants to do—and keep doing. If he comes to class just because you made him, odds are that he won't receive the full benefits yoga has to offer. That is because it is a fully personal experience, and a difficult one that will only take root if the practitioner is sincere.

And a sincere wish to shut you up is not the sincerity we need. I've seen more husbands staring at the clock than I care to admit. I've seen more wives quietly frustrated that their partners are staring at the clock than I like. Even worse, I've seen and heard hushed arguments in class as yoga-wife tries to convince her husband into a posture that he is convinced he will never make. In those instances, the experience is ruined for them both. (And for me, taking charge of that in a class is straight up awful.)

The very best way to persuade a stubborn man to experience yoga is to simply live by example. Continue on with your practice, keeping your attention on what you learn. What you experience. What you discover. Then just take it home with you. He can't help but to be intrigued by your newfound peace and serenity. He can't help but to be a little jealous when you stop sharing complaints about common aches and pains. There may come a point when you manage to demonstrate to him how much better life is with yoga by just simply being who you are.

My mule will never come to a class. I know that without doubt. And at this point, I wouldn't take him to one if he begged. I refuse to sympathize with an aching back after years of telling him how to alleviate that same back problem. He gets no "poor baby" from me when he complains of a sciatic problem that has been nagging him for moths. You know what I tell him?

You should have taken up yoga when I told you to. Oddly enough, it was this approach that finally worked. Now he just comes to me and asks for stretches or postures to take care of things that bother him. And I'm alright with that. Because it comes down to the plain fact that you can lead a horse to water, but you can't make him drink.

Same thing goes for mules.

I had a massage not too long ago where I commented to the masseur that I just couldn't fathom why I had such pain in my leg. And he replied (very blithely), "Well, you're an athlete, that's why."

Now, to a girl who more often than not caught the kickball in gym with her face and not her hands, this was an astounding proclamation. I'm no athlete; I'm a yoga instructor. I don't compete. One of my very fundamental teachings is that we don't treat yoga like a sport, it's a practice, an experience. I am the very antithesis of an athlete in all the ways that count.

Or am I?

I've slowly come to realize that anyone who participates in a physical activity with diligence, regularity and joy is an athlete. If you run the streets of Naples and never a marathon, you are still an athlete. If your golf game would make Tiger Woods cringe, but you love it and do it, you are still an athlete. If you play tennis with your grandmother every week and lose, you are still an athlete. Athletics is about participation and attention to the body or to the activity, not necessarily about successful competition. So, in a way, all of us who play are athletes. And that means we are all susceptible to athletic injury.

Frequent participation in a beloved activity often leads to repetitive motion injury, muscle strain and physical imbalances. Sports that involve swinging, such as golf, tennis and baseball, all ask the body to twist and move in a consistently same motion, which can lead to back and shoulder problems. Sports that involve running often create troubles in the ankles, knees and lower back due to the pounding of the feet on the pavement, grass or turf. Activities that require extreme flexibility, such as gymnastics and, yes, even power yoga, can bring about pulled muscles or tendons. You may play your sport for years and never a problem see, but one day, be assured, it will arise. The athletic body needs constant attention. It needs you to give consideration to what you are doing. It needs you to listen and hear even the faint messages of pain or strain that you create when you play.

Many of us just assume that aches and pains are par for the course. And, to some extent, they are. If you use anything the same way frequently, you are simply bound to see some wear. But that doesn't mean there isn't anything you can do about it. A practice of gentle yoga can help balance out these repetitive motion imbalances, create flexibility and fluidity in stiffening joints, ease back pain or strain. It is an athletic supplement par excellance.

Yoga does this by bringing the body back to balance. It teaches you the skills needed to really listen to what the body has to say. It shows you how to create a state of absolute focus. You might just be surprised at what you had never noticed. I won't promise that all of the dings you put in the body after years of hard use will just vanish, but I can assure you that this practice will create a difference in how you feel. In the body, in the mind, in your sport. Every athlete—professional, dilettante, or weekend warrior—deserves the benefits yoga can bring. Yoga is the mate to your activity. The yin to its yang. The Spock to your Kirk. It helps maintain the foundation on which the health of your athletic endeavour grows.

So, no, maybe you'll never be Peyton Manning or Serena Williams. But add yoga to your program and you can continue to pretend for a long, long time.

Watch me, now. I'm going right over to yonder tree and I'm gonna climb right up it. Surely am. And then I'm a-gonna shimmy out onto that skinny, skinny limb and set up my little soapbox. Can y'all hear me down there?

Good.

Many more women than men attend yoga classes. That's a fact. So much so that yoga in the West has come to be associated with the feminine. Yet, this is completely contrary to Eastern yoga, where men dominate. Why is that? Having interviewed a number of average, non-yogi men on the subject I am not surprised to say that the answer is hardly forthright. I have heard everything from, "It's a girlie sport," to "It's too hard." I guess I should have expected no less. So that leaves me to contemplate, speculate, and postulate on this tricky topic alone.

I must conclude, after much deliberation, that I believe Western men do not resonate to yoga largely because there is no immediate achievement and no clear competition. Unlike popular sports, yoga does not give you a competitive rush, or the sense of having "won." No crowd will ever scream madly when you manage a perfect headstand. There is no finish-line tape to burst through when you complete a sun-salutation for the eighty-seventh time. Scoreboards and second clocks do not exist in yoga. So how does a man know if he's faster, stronger, smarter—better— than the next?

I think that's the hurdle for many modern men. Yoga is not a sport, although it demands considerably more than any mere athletic event. Yoga can be physically tough. It can be the most challenging mental and physical exercise you will ever come across. A hard practitioner could go toe to toe with any athlete in terms of focus, endurance and strength. Male or female.

However, there is no clear-cut method for determining your yoga "success," or any playbook that lays down how and when you will complete the task. Yoga demands patience and reflection, steadiness and fortitude. Achievement happens over a lifetime. Competition has no place. Mayhap this is too confusing to our common, Western male.

When spirituality for men comes in Bud Lite ads, and accomplishment races around a track at 140 mph, how can yoga hope to capture their hearts? Everything that we teach our young males comes wrapped in competition. So much so that success is only measured by the vanquishing of another. Our heroes are those who have exercised this methodology in its most complete sense: Corporate sharks, cut-throat tycoons, ruthless lawyers, professional athletes.

This type of thinking will never raise its head in yoga. Never. So its really no wonder that your average Joe Friday man won't bother with it. We've taught him that it has no value.

The only person to compete with in yoga is yourself, and the only foe you will ever conquer is your ego. This is true in all of life whether we want to admit it or not. But most people, most men, don't understand the value of this way of thinking. It is simply not the way they were raised. Do better. Beat them. Prove that you are the best and therefore more worthy. Of what? Don't ask me. I'm missing the Y chromosome and all of its sundry parts.

I could be very wrong. It could also be that men sense the daring and difficulty of yoga and are afraid of pitting their "superior" athleticism against women. Especially in a practice that has, somehow, come to be dominated by them.

Oh, dear. Was that a gauntlet that just fell from my tree limb?

A few weeks ago, a gentleman came to class. An experienced yogi, he had brought his father to a beginner class in an effort to share the benefits of Yoga. Despite his advanced level, he practiced as a beginner to encourage another to try. It was lovely to behold. But as they left, I overheard a bit of their conversation. (I know, I know…eavesdropping bad. Bad teacher! Bad!) The father asked how this class differed from others, and the son replied, "My other instructor pays more attention to detail."

Well, that's what I get for eavesdropping, right? Let me tell you, I went right up into smoke. "Details? He thinks I don't pay attention? He thinks I'm a bad instructor! He thinks I don't know what I'm doing! Wait, do I know what I am doing?! Am I wrong??!! Oh, no. I am wrong. I'm terrible!" The insecurities roared out of me like Dragon's breath until I remembered something. Something precious and simple.
The Devil, they say, is in the details. And the details can lock you up faster than US41 in season.

Yoga is perceived and taught in many different ways. And, he's right. I am not a detail instructor. I wasn't taught that way and I don't practice that way. But that does not make me a bad instructor. On the contrary. I am a big believer in the yoga experience. I would rather see a student experience the lightness of being than the absolutely perfect posture. Because, in my experience, when you enmire yourself completely in the tiny, nitty details of the physical, you lose the ebb and flow of greater connection. To tune in only to the detail is to concern oneself with the mundane and to lose the cosmic.

People will disagree. And that's their prerogative.

But I think some practices focus so deeply on the detail of the physical that everything gets distilled down into body awareness. This provides a great sense of focus. But it doesn't allow for that unique sense of yogic release when the mind is sharp, the spirit connects and the body just flows. I know that I can't really let go when I am concerned with engaging the shoulder loop, internal rotation of the upper thigh bone and external rotation of the lower leg, one hip rolling out to press the external ridge of the foot down. That just feels busy to me. And you can't imagine what that is like to teach. Every time I try, students look at me as if springs have just popped from my ears and a little yellow cuckoo bird is doing the cha cha off of my tongue. Crazy lady, whachoo talkin' 'bout?

Life is so busy anyway. Why does yoga have to be busy too? Yes, it is important to practice the postures correctly. But correct can be different for every body. If you're cruising in the experience, I don't think I should interrupt unless you are on the path to injury. Believe me, I've got my eye out. I've got you covered. And I will adjust you if it comes to that. But I'm not going to chatter away, hammering you with details that you may or may not understand. Yoga is a deeply private, personal experience between your body, mind and God. It is the path to finding your connection.

I can't draw you a detailed map to get there. I wouldn't even dream to try. All I can do, all any instructor can do, is to guide gently. To illuminate the path you must walk alone. To do more is to make my experience your experience. And that is as dangerous as not paying attention at all.

As they say, The devil is in the details.

101

So many people ask which type of yoga they should practice. They read about this kind of yoga or that; they've heard about Hatha, Astanga, Ama, Sampoorna, Anusara, yada, yada, yada. The list is endless.

Correction: the list isn't endless, its endlessly growing. Somehow, yoga has become infected with the marketing bug. Anyone with a personal spin on this old practice can slap their name on it, wrap it up in a trademarked bow and feed it to the public as "new." Lets hope they never call it "improved."

I think my very heart would melt.

The primary offender, and in my opinion, the worst, is Bikram Choudhury. He is the founder, and leader, of Bikram Yoga®, otherwise known as "hot" yoga.

His practice involves 26 strictly sequenced postures performed in a 105-degree heated room. This to me has always seemed ludicrous. But, there are valid reasonings behind his theory. Bikram proposes that the extreme heat actually prevents the body from overheating while protecting the muscles from damage. This makes a certain amount of sense if one considers that heat relaxes muscles, therefore allowing one to work through the postures to the fullest extent. He also claims that the heat will detoxify the body while allowing the pores to open and release these toxins. Again, anyone who has ever had a facial can attest to the validity of this. The heat will thin the blood, cleansing the circulatory system. We all know, as residents of hot Florida, that this is also true. His strict sequencing of postures has roots in solid logic, as well. Any good instructor follows a sequence of postures, whether they are the same postures every class or not. That is just the way of yoga. Certain poses should be practiced before others. In this way the body, and the mind, is properly prepared for a full practice. Bikram has chosen 26 postures that he feels comprises a complete practice. Now, that, I believe, is a matter of opinion.

Many people swear by this practice. They claim it is the best way to a full and satisfying yoga "workout." There are legions of Bikram practitioners all over the world that are happy, happy, happy with their practice. Good for them.

So, having said all of that, let me add: Are you kidding me? You cannot trademark yoga! How dare you! Yoga is a deeply personal experience that is, by its nature, chameleon like. It changes everyday. Just as you change everyday. How can you think that 26 postures will suit you all the time? How can that be enough when there are more than 600 postures to choose from? The notion that a practice should be the same day after day makes me cringe. It's naive. Worse than that, it is to invite static into your practice, to remove the processes of change from your practice when change is what we are all seeking to achieve. Change is evolution. It is nature.

Furthermore, that particular level of heat strikes me as over the top. I'm all for warming the body before practice, but that can be achieved through breath and asana. One hundred and five degrees is way beyond the point where newscasters start announcing "heat-index" warnings. As in, don't go outside or exert yourself warnings, you just might die. So, great, lets lock ourselves in a tiny room with 20 other people and exercise. That's a brilliant idea. My response to the Bikram question is this: You live in Florida. If you like it hot, go outside and do 26 postures on the beach at noon in August. Just don't call it Bikram.

You might get sued.

Like little lambs in the wood, we wander unprepared into cold and flu season. Many will be lulled by a false sense of security, believing that the simple fact that we live in a warm climate will protect us from the harsh brunt of winter weather illnesses. Not so, not so.

If anything, our climate makes us even more susceptible to varied types of disease. Family, friends and visitors soar in from far and wide on those giant flying Petri dishes known as airplanes, bringing different, varied strains of any number of viruses. Then they hug us, shake our hands, share their tainted cash and touch everything in sight, spreading, spreading, spreading colds and flu. It is a bit scary when you think about the vastness of it.

There are, of course, any number of ways to protect yourself. From hand washing, to anti-bacterial gels to flu shots, you do not have to succumb to disease. It is not inevitable. But there are a few more things you can do to improve the health of your immune system of which you may not be aware. Ridiculously obvious things that you should do anyway, cold and flu season or not.

For instance, did you know that the health of your immune system is directly affected by the amount of happiness or stress in your life? The body's adrenaline response to stress actually lowers the number of Immune cells present at work. This weakens the immune system and prevents us from effectively fighting off disease. Furthermore, this weakened state makes us feel less productive and creative, sucking the energy right out of our bodies. Like a vicious circle, this can create more stress because we feel that we cannot accomplish all that we need to. So, in a nutshell, relax. It will keep you from getting sick.

If you do your best to handle things as they come, instead of putting them off or burying them beneath denial, you will empower yourself—as well as your immune system. A simple change of perspective can prevent those nasty viruses from getting a hold of you and working their evil magick. If you allow yourself to wallow in frustration, anger, helplessness or sorrow, you let go of your own spiritual power and open up the door to stress. Again. These negative feelings drain your energy and place you in the role of the victim. And are you ever more of a victim than when you fall prey to sickness?

Feeling in control of your life will keep you out of this cycle. If you take responsibility for your actions, accept your mistakes and change your focus to the positive, you will be filling your system with energy. This selfsame energy strengthens the whole body, emotional, physical, and spiritual. There is nothing then that you cannot handle or conquer. Including disease. So if you actively cultivate joy, gratitude and unity, you are helping to keep these viruses at bay.

And, finally, for the love of Pete, have some fun. Laugh and make merry. Be creative for no other reason than you feel like it. Hang out with your friends and do nothing of consequence at all. Tell stupid jokes. Doodle silly pictures with crayon. Don't feel like you have to explain the validity of this to anybody. You don't have to. Lightness is it's own reward. Joy and health walk hand in hand.

'Tis the season, kiddies. Be vigilant. And remember, of course, take all of the obvious precautions—eat well, get plenty of vitamins and minerals, keep your hands clean, etc.—but also try to be well in the mind and heart. It might just tip the scales in your favor for a illness free season.

103

I would lay odds that at some point during the course of your childhood, your mother, father, grandmother, so on, said to you, "If you keep making that face, it'll get stuck that way."

And you laughed it off. We all do. Ha! Its quite an awakening the day you realize that every expression ever made has slowly carved its way into the skin of your face, leaving a road map of your past joys and sorrows. But such is the nature of life.

An entire market has been birthed to combat this. Botox, Alpha-hydroxy, plastic surgery, all developed to combat the signs of aging. But is aging the sole problem? Or is it also that we wear the same expression on our face all day every day, and, lo and behold, it got stuck?

Few of us give a passing thought to the neutral expressions our faces assume when we aren't laughing or crying. Our features just settle home and rest. But this neutral expression tells more than a few of our secrets. There are those who always seem to have a 'sour puss' as my grandmother would put it, wearing their disappointments for the whole world to see. Whether they realize it or not, this puss is imprinting itself onto the features. It is manifesting a face presented to the world.

My laugh lines are cherished. The furrow over my brow not so much. Those are honestly owned and willingly shared. It's the unconscious frown I find sometimes when I'm working that demonstrates my point. That's not something I want to present to others right out of the gate. People react to first impressions. They make judgments based on very little actual information, deciding quickly what kind of person you are. For good or bad, this is just true. The tone of voice, the set of your shoulders, the posture of the body, the expression of the face all contribute lightning quick to a person's perception of you.

What is your face sharing without your consent?

As it happens, I know a yoga breathing technique to combat this. (Really? No! You don't say!) Leave it to those yogis to think of everything.... Make a "C" shape out of your left hand. Then lay the pad of the thumb between the top and middle knuckle of the forefinger. Now, wrap the fingers of right hand around the top of the left fingers,

laying the right thumb next to the left one. You have a very loose fist, like a tunnel made out of the hands.
With the thumbs next to one another, you should see a natural 'hole' between the bottom and middle knuckles. Bring this hole about twelve inches away from the mouth and slightly lower. Inhale through the nose, long and slow. Then exhale through the mouth, blowing like you would blow a kiss. Blow right through that hole, long and slow. Close they eyes and breathe deeply, slowly and consciously. In through the nose, out through the lips. You should hear the breath traveling through the hands like a low, soft whistle. Exactly like wind blowing gently through a tunnel.

This exercise will make you feel calm and happy and bring an easy expression to the face. It is not recommended mid day, or when you have work to do, as it will also make you feel very relaxed and maybe even a little sleepy. But if you practice this regularly, Yogi Bhajan says that your face will become charming and innocent.

Whether or not you think that is a good thing is up to you. But I'll take that over frown lines any day of the week.

The benefits of a yoga practice are far-reaching and wide. Some are obvious. They are the primary motivations for beginning—or maintaining—your practice. Flexibility, strength, focus and stress relief are all examples of this primary motivation. But the practice of yoga offers a number of periphery benefits that you may not be aware of. Think of them like interest on your checking account. Good to have, but hardly the reason you signed on.

My favourite of these benefits is the ability to easily fall asleep and to sleep well. I believe this to be the result of the mind training that we do in yoga. As you practice you are forever being reminded to clear the mind and let idle chatter fall away. This results in the ability to be aware when your mind is running away and to pull it back. I can't think of any time that skill would be more valuable than when you are lying wide awake, held hostage by a monkey mind that won't let you drift off.

According to the innumerable pharmaceutical advertisements, this is the primary factor in sleeplessness. Sleeping pills and I do not mix well, so I will claim a bias here. For those of you who really believe that you need them, please don't come chasing after me with a stick when I say that I don't think you ever really need them. If restless mind is the primary reason that people can't fall asleep, then I feel pretty confident telling you that I know another way that won't have you flirting with addiction.

Undertaking a complete yoga program is one way. I believe it is the best, and most comprehensive method to bring your life to a point where sleep is not something you worry about. But then, I would. For some of you, that is not a realistic option. So, I say to thee, here is one yoga technique that will help you still the mind enough to find the elusive slumber.

Alternate nostril breath is remarkably calming. It can be done sitting up, or, if you are in bed, lying down. Bring your right palm in front of your face. Make the peace sign, or the Victory "V". Now bring the forefinger and middle finger tightly together. Press these two fingers between the eyebrows just above the eyebrow ridge. Now release the thumb and ring finger to rest on alternate sides of the nose—thumb to right nostril, ring finger to left nostril. Inhale. Pinch the right nostril shut with the thumb. Not hard enough to push the nose over! Just enough to block the nostril. Exhale out of the left nostril. Inhale through the same nostril then pinch the left shut with the ring finger, release the thumb and exhale right. Inhale right, pinch, exhale left. Inhale left, pinch, exhale right. Keep the breath long and slow, flowing in and out of each nostril in turn. You will notice a calm bliss settle over you as the mind becomes engrossed with the task and releases whatever it was that kept it churning so intently.

If you want to take it even deeper, add a silent mantra of "Sat Nam". Inhale Sat, exhale Nam. If that doesn't work for you and your faith, "Amen" works just as well. Inhale Ah, exhale Men. This brings the vibration of the divinity into your mind. And I don't think worries about taxes, work, relationships, money, etc. stand a chance when pitted against that. Do you?

Start here. And if this works, expand. Allowing some yoga into your life, even if it is the tiniest amount, can refresh and rejuvenate. If good sleep is considered a side benefit, can you only imagine what the primary perks are like?

105

I rarely, if ever, gush. It's true, ask anyone who truly knows me. When it comes to expressing my personal partialities, I am practically British in my reservedness. I can't explain why, but when I really, really, *really* like something, I tend to keep it to myself.

So mark it when I say to you: If you only ever listen to one thing that I say, let it be this. If you are curious but doubtful of yoga, try this. If you don't think you can manage the physical practice of yoga but want to experience its peace, try this. If you are trapped in a quagmire of personal life difficulties and are seeking a path to resolution, try this. You must, must, must try Yoga Nidra.

It is one of the most remarkable things I have ever done. Or, not done as the case may be.

They call yoga nidra "yogic sleep" and every yoga class has a shadow of yoga nidra in it. That final relaxation, where you lie comfortably on your back and drift away is a pale remembrance of this powerful, peace-inspiring practice. Yoga nidra is like that final Savasana only a thousand times richer. It is true, unimpeded relaxation. Wow.

Imagine, if you will, the last time you fell asleep absolutely certain that all was well with the world. That everything was within your understanding and that all was exactly as it should be. Can you even remember a time when your busy mind did not try to sort things out, to shuffle them into some sort of order before your body found respite? Were you but a child the last time you experienced that deep level of trust that allowed you to truly rest? When was the last time you drifted off with peace and not from simple exhaustion?

This malaise is a symptom of our imbalances within duality. We accept that everything has a natural opposite—and that is very true. It is the nature of nature. But we deny that all opposites are but one. That everything is One. Happiness and Sadness are but two sides of the same coin. One is not better than the other and you cannot have one without the other. It is impossible to know Happy without Sad, or Trust without Fear. And, therefore, you cannot assign 'good' to one and 'bad' to the other. They all have their place.

If we constantly seek to be only happy then we throw ourselves out of balance with nature. If we only recognize pleasure and ignore pain then we can never learn. We will forever be seeking and never finding the peace and understanding of One Unifying Force. It is this one that holds all twos together. It is not up to us to pick and choose between them.

This is a foundation principle of Yoga Nidra. It is this thinking that allows you to abandon the neverending quest for all that is happy and perfect and to simply be. Let everything be what it is. Be, even for just a moment, with the One. Goodness, how liberating. Gracious, how relaxing. Its really Okay, I promise.

So please, hear me. Even if it is only for this brief instant. YOGA NIDRA. Its fantastic. Its beyond fantastic. Give it a try. You can thank me later.

You cannot imagine how many times a week I hear, "My (body part) does this funny thing when I do (insert movement here). Are there specific exercises I should be doing at home?" This type of inquiry is remarkably common, seeing as how most people come to yoga for relief from one ailment or another. As a matter of fact, yoga in the west is usually seen as being only a prescriptive practice, or, in simple terms, just plain good for what ails ya.

Generally, I don't mind answering these kinds of questions, or reinforcing the belief that yoga is simply this. It is the first step, and any first step—no matter how simplistic—is always good. I know that eventually, should this student continue to practice, the next set of questions will be the ones that I really want to hear. It is an inevitability that once someone really starts living with yoga that they will discover that it is so very much more than a simple 'cure' for physical ailments. And nothing makes me happier than a student asking, "How can I create a home practice?" Oh, purrrrrr……

This is when I usually set them in front of the studio library and tell them to pick something, anything, to read. There is a ton of great yoga literature out there—some better than others—that will help a seeker move beyond forward folds and backbends and into the philosophy of why we do forward folds and backbends. There are really interesting, and remarkably simple texts on the nature of the mind and the use of asana to find peace and happiness within. One good book, one right book, can catapult a student out of the simple realms of yoga and into the realms of true self-exploration.

If I'm really lucky, said student returns and then asks about deepening this personal practice. This indicates that he/she has begun to develop a relationship with yoga and that it is slowing working its way into their hearts, minds and, ultimately, into the processes of their thoughts. And once yoga has made an inroad into the way one thinks, true alchemy begins to happen. Lives begin to change.

Delightfully, the process of developing a true personal practice is not something that can be proscribed. It is an intimate relationship as sacred as the one you have with a lover, a relationship that is intensely individual. When it comes to developing this relationship the best I can do is tell you this: pay attention to it. Nurture it. Take time every day to explore something about it and learn what it means for you.

Your personal practice—that which happens outside of class—can be anything from a few moments of insightful reflection to a full, sweaty hour of pretzel twisting. Hopefully, it will end up being both. There is no one answer. The very best thing you can do when creating this relationship is to let it come. Without expectation, let it come to you as it wants. In this way it will be pure. It will represent your personal connection to the godforce. If you have been studying yoga in any manifestation, you must trust that you have the necessary foundation.

Just sit still and get quiet. Then listen. Let your body flow with whatever movements rise up. Let yourself meditate if that is what the day requires. Breathe, and let this breath lead you where you need to go. You already have the answers you need. You just have to uncover them.

And if all that arises from a simple inquiry about tight hips, then God bless. Ask away.

As you can possibly well imagine, I am most often asked about relaxation. As a yoga instructor, it is immediately assumed that I know some secret, that I have been initiated into a relaxation cult and that there is some magic incantation somewhere, known only to the tribe of yogi.

While I would love to say that this is all true, the plain fact of the matter is that there is no magic 'trick' to bring about relaxation. Like practically everything else in life, relaxation is something that one makes time for, and something that one must dedicate attention to. It is an outlook, an attitude. A choice.

True, lasting relaxation is not about having time to sit in front of the TV with a beer, or lugging yourself down to the beach, or wandering through the mall. These things, while somewhat satisfying, are mere distractions from the path of enduring relaxation. Walking this path is a practice, an effort, an awareness of being. Relaxation is a state of grace and balance. A place from which all things can flow. It is peace of heart.

That is probably not what you were expecting to hear. You may have expected me to just come up here and say, do this, do that and ye shall be relaxed. Wooga-booga, shanthi, shanthi; I make thee stress free. Would that it were that easy. If it were, I'd be very rich and you all would walk out of here with lasting, eternal bliss. But, alas....

There are no absolute answers. Each body is unique. Each spirit is unique. Every day is different. But having an awareness of that is one step to finding peace. Letting go of perfection and connecting to what is, is another. Taking the time to look for things like awareness and connection in your life is the foundation on which a peaceful outlook is built.

It is work. But it is glorious, valuable, good work that inspires rather than drains, refreshes rather than tires, relaxes rather than stresses. There are, of course, things that we do in yoga that help that process along. There is a reason that yoga has been continually practiced for over 5000 years. The postures and philosophy are a broad, well traveled road to lasting peace and connection. We do have practices that can bring about an instant state of calm. Certain breaths and postures can cool the mind immediately, dismissing stress like a noisome mosquito.

These exercises can inspire peace, stop time, and cure insomnia. But as we move through them, I want you to remember the importance of the depth behind the practice. This primary understanding: you must always connect to the exercise, to fully understand what you are doing, why you do it, and how it makes you feel. To merely do something because I tell you it will help you relax is foolish. I could just as easily tell you that a martini will do the trick, or a valium. The point here is to always cultivate self- awareness. To fully inhabit your space and know what it going on within it.

Once this is cultivated, a light is turned on and life is lived illuminated. You can more clearly see things that cause stress, recognize when you are moving into stress, understand that you have the power to release it. But if you don't know how to do that, if you live life disconnected, if you wander through your days with your mind three steps ahead of you, you create space for things to move in and hide. Things like stress, sickness, apathy. Presence is your strongest weapon in the battle for peace.

Many of us rush along, assuming that certain things will just work on their own, like a clock. Our bodies, our hearts, our breath. These things are rarely thought about unless they speak up, until they start to protest and our awareness is drawn to them. Some people will live their entire lives without knowing what it means to really flex the body, to get the heart singing, or to fill the soul with air. Somewhere within, we know the value of these things. But, oh how easily they are forgotten. How sadly they are ignored. And what a price many of us ultimately pay for not attending to them.

In that vein, before we move on, I need for you all to understand what it means to breathe. I need you to feel the value of true, eternal breath. Take a deep breath and sigh it out. Just let it go. Inhale. Sigh. Where did that breath go in the body? I'd lay odds that it went directly into your chest. Do it again, and pay attention. Where did the breath go? How did it make you feel?

Breathing into the chest is an old and bad habit most of us learned from who knows where. It is a half breath, a fight-or-flight response gone awry and turned into habit. To truly breathe, one must employ the entire system. The breathing mechanism actually begins in the belly, low down. Completely relax the tummy, letting go of the natural "suck it in" that most of us do without even thinking about it. As you inhale allow the belly to grow full and round, like a balloon until it is so full that you feel the breath spill over into the ribcage and the chest. Slowly, taking to time to experience the fullness of the belly, to find the full circumference of the ribcage and the small spaces between the ribs. Discover room beneath the breastbone and between the chest muscles. Fill it all up, luxuriously slow. Take your time and breathe.

Good. Now, how did that breath make you feel? How was it different from the one before? Knowing how to breathe allows us to work with the breath, modifying it, directing it, creating a tool to promote health and abolish stress.

The first breath 'tool' is called Alternate nostril breathing. It is a fantastic remedy to stress, and an excellent way to crush insomnia. It is used to balance out the nervous system, to open up the "nadis" or energy channels that traverse the body like a giant power grid. This system is critically attached to the spine in that without the spine there is no connection or communication throughout the body. Your spine is a nexus of energy and nerves. It is the primary channel that connects us to heaven and earth, and your powerhouse of vitality. Your spine is your very best friend and the single part of your body you should honour and exercise above all else. Keeping the spine, and all of its connections healthy, is fundamental to fully exploring peace and longevity.

Visualize the spine as a brilliant conduit of energy, from the tail to the third eye point, or the point between the eyebrows and behind the forehead. This third eye point is the place in which we explore the mind, connecting it not only to the body, but to the greater identity. Twisted around this conduit are two other channels, representing masculine and feminine energies, not unlike a DNA helix. From the tail they twine around and around, terminating at the nose, directly beneath the third eye. By alternating the breath between nostrils, we can bring balance to these forces, clear out any garbage hiding out in the core system and bring calmness to the mind.

To begin, bring the first two fingers of the right hand up against the third-eye point, or the space just above the space between your brows.

Set the thumb against the right nostril and the ring finger up against the left. Once you have exhaled through a nostril, you will inhale through the same nostril before switching and moving on. Easy, now, block off the right nostril and inhale left. Switch, blocking the left nostril and releasing the right to exhale slowly through the right. Inhale right, switch, exhale left. Inhale left, switch, exhale right. Do this for about three minutes.

Take a moment now to listen to what has happened in your body. Notice the differences between this moment and before you started. Feel the quality of your breath, be aware of what it does to your body and mind, hear the spirit sighing its thanks.

For, yes, while this is a practical exercise, with roots in physical understanding, it is also an exercise in self-awareness. It is you, stepping back from life to be with yourself for just a moment. For this time you have dedicated yourself to your own body, to your own mind, and to your own peace. Noting else mattered and your attention was rooted, grounded, still. You were connected to the simple flow of breath and everything else drifted away.

That is how you beat stress. By simply putting it away. Begin to make choices that put you at the center of your life. And while that may sound selfish, it is absolutely not. For if you are not healthy, if you are not present—fully present and aware—what good are you? This exercise took three minutes. The sky did not fall, the earth did not tremble from your absence. But you, you moved into yourself, you paid full attention to yourself and your care and took one step closer to heaven. *Now* you can share that peace with someone you know. Or better yet, with someone you don't know. Being here, being connected and aware leaves stress out in the cold.

Remember this feeling. Set it as a bookmark. When you start to spin out, pull yourself back to this place. Take a breath. Take two, take three. There is always time if you believe it to be so.

Now, sometimes you won't be in a place where you feel comfortable with the Alternate nostril breath. Granted, it would be a little hard to perform in the car, with a kid on the hip, or on a sales floor. But that doesn't mean that you have to accept stress simply because your hands are busy.

Moving into a 1:4 breath will give you similar benefits. On a purely physical level, this breath keeps more oxygen in the body for a longer period of time. The understanding being that the more oxygen in the system, the richer the blood. The richer the blood, the greater its ability to nourish. Nourish the body, the brain, the mind, and yes, even the spirit.

This is, quite simply, a complete breath performed in the ratio of one to four. One long count to inhale, four long counts to exhale. Go ahead, close the eyes and give it a try.

This is great if you need to be innocuous, or if you want to breathe privately in a public place. This 1:4 breath forces you to focus, to be still, to move into primary awareness. Where are you? What are you doing? How do you feel? The mind quiets and you can see clearly that which brings you stress. You can look it in the eye and disengage. Even if you have to return to the stressful situation, you don't have to accept the stress of it.

Your breath is a weapon and an ally the likes of which you have never known.

All you have to do is tap it.

So, here you came to learn how to relax and all I've told you to do is breathe. Heard that before? As I said, there is no magic ingredient or incantation. It all boils down to breath and intent. It all boils down to awareness. It can be as serious a practice as you need it to be, or as irreverent.

Much of the stressors in our lives are those we put upon ourselves. Our market-driven, social belief is that we are all supposed to be Cinderella and the fairy godmother combined, and many of us have agreed to cram our feet into her little glass slippers. We then march around town, doing everything we can to be perfect and productive, stoutly ignoring the fact that those shoes don't fit. Stress in life comes from ignoring that which is true to ourselves, that which is organic and natural and feminine. I say, step-sisters unite! Kick off those blister-causing slippers and be free!

Getting rid of them can be so simple as to be ridiculous. Just as letting go of that which does not serve you or your highest purpose is within the realm of possibility.

We live in the great "melting pot" , when we should live in a beautiful mosaic. That which is unique is quickly melted down and stripped of its precious individuality. Our modern ideals are of those of freedom and liberty and individuality—as long as they fit in the pot. As long as they don't rock the boat. When did we come to accept that?

Look around, this is our life. This is what we have chosen to accept.

What immense stress that alone puts on our lives! But living in awareness can combat that. We do not have to live consumed by what we ought to be doing, how we ought to appear, what we ought to think and believe. Most of us just stoutly swim along in the rushing river of American living, just trying to keep our heads above water, never thinking that we have the power to swim ourselves to shore. That we have the ability to make the change.

That is painfully and utterly ludicrous. There is no "ought". There is no judgement but that which we accept and own. You can refuse the stress of this as easily as you accept it. You are welcome to sit on the river bank and watch the drowning rats rush by. You are free to call out words of encouragement to them as I do to you right now.

It is time to find our own way. To live a life of deep breaths, worthy moments & great humour. Life is, by its very nature, absurd. It is, in my experience, more like an existential episode of Hee-Haw than it is Sense and Sensibility. So, hell, lets roll with it. Lets laugh at it loudly and with as much vulgarity as we can possibly muster.

The singular best method to beating stress is to step back and take a clear look. And then, give it a good laugh. A rollicking, outrageous, inappropriate hoot. I guarantee you, there is a measure of the ridiculous in everything. You can find something to laugh at. Because joy is your right. It is a basic human drive. One that we often forget in the face of "proper living". So let's just go ahead and get rid of that habit right now. Smash those glass shoes with the hammer of frivolity.

It is within your human rights to find joy wherever you can. To sing at the top of your lungs. Dance like an African tribal woman on the front lawn. Go barefoot to work. Wear loud clothes and boisterous jewelry. One of my favourite ways to relax is in the car, oddly enough. I'll put in an old CD from my younger days and sing like I am Paul Simon, or

Dave Matthews. I'll roll all the windows down and turn the music up to the point where I can't hear myself. That's right. I'm the girl playing the steering wheel bongos and strumming the stick shift guitar. I'll share my Paul Simon with the whole wide world, mouth wide open, fingers jammin', body bouncin'. Havin' me a good old time.

And you want to know what? Most people see me and smile. And I say, "pooh!" to those who don't.

Develop the ability to let go. To get over it. To be yourself completely. Or, better yet. Go home and put on some funky music, kick off your shoes and grab a wooden spoon. Roll the neck a few times, shake out the legs and let 'er rip. Dance like there is no tomorrow. Dance like you are calling down the rain. Dance like your ancestors souls depend upon it. There are no mirrors. There is no mating ritual at play. No one is watching. Shake that booty and boogie down with as much freedom as you have within you. Think its silly?

That's the point.

Relaxation isn't a task. Its an expression. A natural state of grace. Relaxation is about being an organic being, free of the modern restraints we strap around our-Selves. Stress is its exact opposite and absolutely controllable without fancy medicines or complicated practices. Feeling "stressed out" is a result of your choices and yours alone. All those things you "have to do" , you chose to do. All of the ideologies or images you follow, you chose to follow. The question becomes, did you make these choices out of awareness, or habit?

Only you can break that mold. Only you can abolish bad habits and find new ones. You are a resourceful, generous, creative, amazing, fantastically original creature with infinite possibility and choice. Find that which does not serve you and I guarantee you will find the majority of the stressors in your life. Don't be afraid to let them go, even if it seems scary. For it is only by cleaning out the old that we make room for the new.

Be bold. Be brave. Be yourself. Take a long, deep breath and rest. Don't be afraid to do less, want less, need less. Simplify. There is nothing wrong with caring for yourself and seeing to your own needs. There is nothing wrong with walking while others around you race.

For the truth of the matter is: we are all only tiny, minute pieces of an infinite whole. You do not hold up the sky or spin the world on its axis. All of your material importance is but dust in the cosmos. I find peace in that, and no small measure of humour.

When you finally make that transition, from personal all-importance to universal connection, you have begun the journey to a life more relaxed. But don't just take my word for it. See it and believe it. Breathe it in and laugh. A joyful and peaceful life does not belong exclusively to the tribe of yogi. It is a gift of god to the tribe of man.

Blessings & Namaste.

108
Practice yoga.

That is my final answer.

Oh, wait, what was the question?

Practice yoga. Because in that way there is at least an hour and a half everyday that is absolutely yours. Sorry. Practicing yoga. Unavailable for comment at this time. Yoga is you time. Practicing yoga recharges the batteries of the soul and refreshes the furnace of the body so that you are then able to help others. With it in your day there is always enough you to go around.

Practice yoga. Because yoga is the only act I know that makes time for itself. At the computer, on the phone, in line at the grocery store, yoga finds its way into your life. It allows you to sense when it is time to slow down, breathe or stretch. It shows you when to stand up or when to let it ride. Yoga moves in and makes itself at home, redecorates the spirit house and throws an endless calmness party. Yoga integrates itself seamlessly.

Practice yoga. Because it brightens the light and lets you see what matters. Yoga introduces you to yourself and your deepest and highest beliefs. It shows you that the gifts of peace and goodwill are here every day if you allow them to be. It teaches you how to share them with little more effort than believing that you can. With yoga, every day has the potential to be sacred.

Practice yoga. Because then you will know what it means to breathe. Really breathe, deep and free. You will know the power of one single breath and understand that one breathing man is a force of nature. You will understand that we all have power beyond imagining to speak our minds, help one another, change the world. To breathe is to join, to be aware, to participate in living. To breathe in yoga is to connect.

Practice yoga. Because it revitalizes and soothes. Because it challenges and nurtures. Because it is a sounding board for health and living. Because it is more than headstands and pretzel twists. Practice yoga and speak out about it, loudly and with great force. Practice yoga and be a community that practices yoga. It is up to us to change the course towards healing and love.

Be about caring for yourself and others. Be about integration. Be about the light. Be about the connection.

Be happy. Practice yoga.

Yup. Definitely my final answer.

Yoga.

Manufactured by Amazon.ca
Bolton, ON

35526380R00129